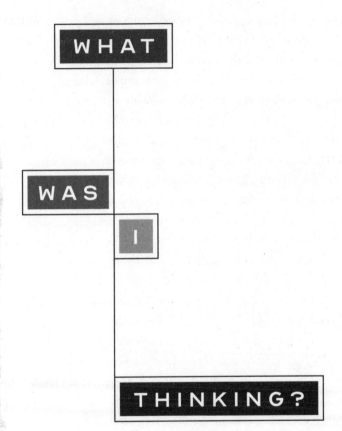

DAVID ASHCRAFT | ROB SKACEL

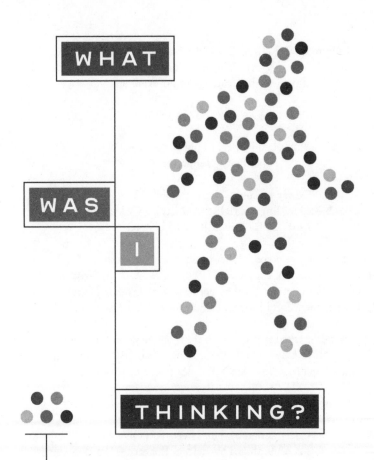

WHAT

WAS

I

THINKING?

HOW TO MAKE BETTER DECISIONS SO YOU
CAN LIVE AND LEAD WITH CONFIDENCE

B&H
PUBLISHING
NASHVILLE, TENNESSEE

978-1-0877-5770-4

Published by B&H Pubishing Group
Nashville, Tennessee

Dewey Decimal Classification: 248.84
Subject Heading: CHRISTIAN LIFE / QUALITY
OF LIFE / DECISION MAKING

Published in association with Wolgemuth & Associates.

Cover design by Tim Green/FaceOut.
Author photos by Jackson Roberts.

1 2 3 4 5 6 7 • 26 25 24 23 22

To our wives, Ruth and Marita,
for encouraging us to risk wisely,
and standing by us in lifelong love.

ACKNOWLEDGMENTS

ACKNOWLEDGMENTS

Thank you to all our friends and family who offered support, encouragement, and assistance with this book.

We are especially thankful for:

Our wives, Ruth and Marita, who both speak truth to us and always have our backs. They've encouraged us to take risks, often expressed more confidence in us than we have in ourselves, and have made it clear that they are beside us and stand behind us no matter what the outcome.

Our teams at LCBC Church and True Edge, who have been willing to work with us and take risks with us, at times while asking the question, "What were you thinking?"

Andrew Wolgemuth and his persistence in finding the right publisher. Taylor Combs and the team at B&H for guiding us through the process.

Peter Greer, for believing our content would be useful to church leaders and for encouraging us to write.

Joelle Walters for her research and conceptual input, and Kim Yarllets for formatting and proofreading help.

Our kids Justin (wife Laura), Ashleigh (husband Kyle), Abe (wife Jordyn), Joelle (husband Caleb), and Eli, who continually take risks by following us and loving us.

CONTENTS

PART 3

FOREWORD

It's been said that, *"Decisions determine destiny."* It's true.

From Adam and Eve's fatal decision to listen to their tempter, to Abraham's decision to listen to the Lord and leave everything behind to follow him to a land he knew nothing about, the long-term consequences of our ancestor's decisions have often far exceeded anything they could have imagined.

That's why our decisions are so important. They don't just impact the immediate moment. They impact the future. And they don't just impact those of us who make the decision. They also impact those we love (and sometimes those we will never meet) in profound and lasting ways.

Granted, while only a few of our decisions will have a massive impact upon the future, and many will have just passing consequences, none are neutral. Every decision we make has consequences.

And therein lies a monumental problem. We can't always know the full spectrum of intended and unintended consequences ahead of time.

Obviously, if we make a decision that we know to be morally wrong or foolish, we shouldn't be surprised when it bears bad fruit. Same with the glaringly obvious decision that bears good fruit. But the fact is, most of our decisions (especially the big ones) are not so easily categorized as right or wrong. They are far more nuanced.

Sometimes it's the choice between the lesser of two evils.

Sometimes it's a choice between good, better, and best.

Sometimes it's a choice between immediate pleasure and long-term consequences.

And almost always, these tougher decisions involve a thing called "risk."

For some of us the easy answer to the risk question is to ALWAYS play it safe. Figure out all the possible negative outcomes and avoid them at all cost. But without taking some appropriate risks (and experiencing some negative consequences along the way) we can never know the sweet fruit of great success. Like someone in Tornado Alley who spends their entire lifetime in a storm shelter, we'll never be hurt by the storm. But we'll also never know the fresh beauty of a spring day.

Then there are those of us who gravitate towards risk. Our fear of missing out and a life of mediocrity is so great that we swing the pendulum in the opposite direction, valuing and pursuing risk as if it's a proper goal in itself, rather than a path that may or may not lead to what we hope for.

Fortunately there is a better way. It's a model for decision-making that David Ashcraft and Rob Skacel spell out in the following pages. They call it DOPE. (I know it's a goofy name, but you'll find it memorable and easy to access.) It provides a valuable path for thinking through those tough decisions that aren't obviously morally right, morally wrong, foolish, or simply a no-brainer.

Obviously, there is no tool or strategy that can guarantee one-hundred percent flawless decision-making. But there are tools and strategies that can greatly increase the odds. And that's what this book provides.

Let's be honest, trusting our gut, doing what we've always done, or what everyone else is doing works most of the time. But the key words are *"most of the time."* Because when they fail, they tend to fail spectacularly, leading to a place I call "Destination Sadness." It's the place where we get everything we wanted only to realize it's not what we wanted. It's the place that leaves us asking that sad age-old question: *"What Was I Thinking?"*

There is a better way. And I'm confident that you will benefit from Ashcraft's and Skacel's decision-making paradigm long after you've finished this book and set it aside.

Dr. Larry Osborne
Teaching Pastor and Kingdom Ambassador
North Coast Church

INTRODUCTION

Thirty-five *thousand*.

A quick search of the internet tells us that's the number of decisions you and I will make in a day. Which means before our eyes have opened each morning, and well before our feet have hit the floor, we are making decisions.

But, even though I know never to doubt the internet, a skeptic like me still has to question that number. Some quick math tells me that 35,000 decisions a day means I would be required to make a decision every 2.5 seconds, 24 hours a day! Though my cynical side says that 35,000 decisions a day seems like a stretch, regardless of the exact number, reality says that you and I are making thousands of decisions each and every day!

- Will I hit snooze? Will I hit it again? How many times can I hit snooze without ruining my day?

- Jeans or yoga pants?
- Do I skip breakfast or pick it up at the drive-through? (According to researchers at Cornell University, we make 226.7 decisions each day on *food alone*.)
- Starbucks or Dunkin?

Some decisions are more involved decisions:

- Do I remind my ten-year-old her science project is due tomorrow?
- Do I express my disappointment (and anger) in my son for once again missing curfew?
- Do I mention to my wife that her car needs to be inspected by end of day tomorrow?
- Cowboys or Eagles?

Then there are life-altering decisions:

- What jobs and career choices will I pursue?
- Who will I date and marry?
- Do I want to have children?
- Democrat, Republican, or Independent?
- What part does God play in my life?
- Am I going to stay in this marriage?

From the moment of birth on into adulthood we share a common desire: the desire of one day having the freedom to make all of our own decisions. But here lies the problem: along with the freedom to make our own decisions come risks. With every decision we make, there are risks.

Risks involve danger, harm, or loss. Risks involve consequences, potentially negative consequences. And many of us were taught as children that we were to avoid risks—perhaps at all costs. We were told to beware of anything that appears risky. We were programmed to associate risks with loss or injury or harm. As a result, we've gone through life believing that risk is bad and carries with it the possibility of something bad happening to us.

> With every decision we make, there are risks.

Add to that the fact that when we have stepped into risks, all too often we find ourselves shaking our heads and asking a far-too-familiar question: *"What was I thinking?"* This confirms our childhood programming and makes us risk-averse.

But that's tragic, because risks are not one-dimensional. Risks are two-sided. Risks involve not only threats, but also opportunities. And in order to reach our full potential in life, we cannot play it safe. We should not completely eliminate risk from our lives, because those reluctant to take risks rarely experience life to its fullest.

Thus the dilemma: How do we learn to make wise decisions in the face of risks? How do we move forward when confronted with uncertainty about the future? Is it possible to learn to take calculated risks and in turn lessen our exposure to danger, harm, or loss?

The reality is that we already take risks every day, and we quite happily do so. Daily we choose to do things we know involve risks. For example, we know that there is risk involved in driving a car. But we accept this risk because in our minds, although the potential consequences could involve death or serious injury, we think that if we are careful, the chances of something dreadful happening are very low.

So, there is a bit of cognitive dissonance. We *think* that risk is inherently bad and to be avoided, but we *act*—often intuitively—as though it were necessary. And it is. Intuitively we know that risks are necessary to bring about success in life. And aversion to risk produces mediocrity.

So this raises a big question: How do we weigh risk and reward? How do we make wise decisions with regard to risk?

We believe it is possible to make better decisions. We can learn to take calculated risks and thus minimize our losses. We can live and lead with confidence. Fortunately, every exposure to risk does not have to end with that same tormenting question, *"What was I thinking?"* It is possible for us to learn how to take calculated risks.

● ● ●

Often, when it comes to making good decisions, the best advice we are given is to simply "Trust your gut!" This sounds great, but what does it even really mean?

In my (David) first thirty years of serving in various church leadership positions, a great deal of thought went into my decisions. Risks were not taken lightly. But I was never able to quantify or explain my decisions.

Time and time again, as our organization moved from one risk-taking venture to another, we would conclude, "Let's go with David's gut on this one!" Which really meant, "We don't have a clue how David came to this conclusion, but because he's made good decisions in the past, we're going to trust David's gut again!"

As our church grew, relying on my gut served us well—that is, until our church grew too big. The organization had outgrown my gut. With more staff and more church attendees, I no longer had all the information available to make the good gut decisions I had grown accustomed to making. Valuable time was wasted and opportunities were missed as our team waited to see what "David's gut was feeling about this situation." Quickly, our team began to realize we were in need of more people who could make good gut-level decisions.

Honestly, I had become a bottleneck to the organization as it waited for my decisions. And as the church grew, I no longer knew all the facts about every ministry or department, making it even more difficult for me to make good decisions and less likely that my gut would be correct!

• • •

In leadership circles, there is a never-ending question about leaders: Are leaders born or are leaders made? The debate is over whether it is possible to learn and grow and develop into a strong leader that others will follow, or whether one must be fortunate enough to be born with these abilities?

Not surprisingly, when it comes to assessing risks and making wise decisions, a similar question exists: Are good decision makers made or are they born with a good gut? Is it possible to learn and grow and develop into a strong and wise decision maker, or must one be fortunate enough to be born with a special gut? Is the ability to take wise and calculated risks available to all people, or is it an ability reserved for a chosen few?

With that question in mind, and out of necessity for more and better decision makers within our organization, I reached out to a friend and former colleague, Dr. Rob Skacel. Rob is a business psychologist with years of experience in helping businesses and churches with organizational development and improved performance. Together, Rob and I began exploring how to teach leaders to develop a gut for good decision-making.

Quickly it became apparent that making wise decisions is not as much a gut instinct as it is a skill—which means that a good decision maker need not be born with a superior gut, but can gain and develop and nurture and even excel at the skill of making good decisions and taking wise risks.

But not only did we want to learn how to help leaders develop the skill of making good decisions; we also had interest in discovering what causes leaders to make bad decisions and take foolish risks. What causes someone who has been so successful at taking risks and who has a history of making great decisions, to all of a sudden take a foolish risk that often destroys their ability to lead and leaves them asking the question, *"What was I thinking?"*

With great frustration we wanted to know: Why do good, proven, seasoned leaders take such foolish risks? And is it possible not only to pass on the skill of good decision-making and wise risk-taking to other leaders, but also to teach leaders the skill of avoiding foolish and destructive risks?

Bottom line: it is our belief that good decision-making and wise risk-taking are skills that can be broken down and refined until a leader excels at taking risks. And we dream about what churches and other organizations would look like if they were led by leaders who have developed the skill of making strong gut-level decisions. How much more could we advance the spread of the good news of Jesus Christ if more leaders were able to make good decisions and were willing to take wise risks? And how much heartache and how many setbacks might be avoided?

But you may have picked up this book to learn to make better decisions, and now are thinking, *I'm not a leader. Will this book help me?* That's the other great news we discovered as we explored these questions about risk and decision-making: anyone can become a great decision maker. It's not just about taking the right risks to advance an organization you lead, but taking the right risks in life, knowing when the reward is worth the risk, and when to take or pass on certain opportunities. If you're not leading a church or other organization, don't put this book down—it's for you too!

So together, let's jump into making better decisions. Let's learn the ingredients to developing a gut that is good at taking wise risks, and avoiding foolish ones.

PART 1

CHAPTER 1

"WHAT WAS I THINKING?"

What was I thinking?" is a question seldom asked on the heels of making a great decision, but it's often the first question asked when a decision goes wrong. And it's a question I (David) have asked myself hundreds of times over the course of my life.

My first recollection of asking that question came in high school. "*What was I thinking?*" I asked myself as I waited for her to answer my call. To me, she was one of the most beautiful and mysterious girls in our high school. Two weeks earlier I had called her. I had asked her out to dinner and a movie. And to my surprise, she had said yes.

This was to be my first real date. And I was petrified. As the time for our date neared, I started feeling sick at my stomach. "*What was I thinking?*" The risks were enormous. *She's out of my league,* I thought. *Besides, I've never been on a date before. What will we talk about?* The risk of being highly embarrassed was too much for me to bear. So I did what any big, strong, not-so-confident teenage boy would do: I backed out!

Sheepishly I left my family sitting at the dining room table and I walked to the back bedroom—as far away as I could be from the rest of my family. With the door closed and sitting on my parents' bed I dialed her number. When she answered, I gave her some lame excuse as to why I needed to cancel our date. Fortunately, she was gracious to me. And as I hung up the phone, once again I asked myself, *"What was I thinking?"*

My second recollection of asking the question was also in high school. We were into cars—muscle cars. Mine was a blue 1967 GTO. We would spend our Friday and Saturday nights driving the streets, acting tougher than we were, and looking for someone to race.

Most weekend nights I would arrive home around 2:00 a.m. and find my parents sitting on the couch, just waiting for me to walk in the door. Each night, their questions were the same: "Where have you been? What have you been doing?" And, "What good could you possibly be up to while being out until 2:00 a.m.?"

Truthfully, we weren't usually doing much of anything. We were driving up and down Forest Lane while complaining about having to pay 33 cents for a gallon of gas. Or we were hanging out in the parking lot at Jack in the Box with hundreds of other teens. And occasionally we would race another muscle car. Most often, we were just dreaming about what might be.

One night, after a dangerous game of cat and mouse while racing a '66 GTO with a custom paint job with the words, *"Purple Haze"* written across the front fender, I lay in my bed while shaking my head in disbelief and asking myself the question, *"What was I thinking?"* Because until that very moment, in the midst of my youthful ignorance, never had the consequences or the risks of racing down a freeway with a car full of my friends ever even crossed my mind.

Variations of that question would follow me throughout college, then grad school and on into my first grown-up job as a camp director. *"What were you thinking?"* the voice asked on the other end of the phone. It was the voice of an exasperated mother of a nine-year-old girl, a camper who had fallen and broken her wrist while participating in a relay race on an obstacle course that I had designed.

"What were you thinking?" asked another caller. This time it was the voice of a frustrated father of a ten-year-old camper. This camper was suffering from heat exhaustion—brought on by that same relay race, on that same obstacle course, that eventually netted three broken wrists and multiple cases of heat exhaustion in less than an hour.

I know what I was thinking. As a brand new, twenty-two-year-old camp director, I was thinking about smiling, laughing campers. I was thinking about campers full of joy and enthusiasm as they participated in activities I had organized. And I was thinking about campers whose lives would be different, campers whose lives might even be changed for eternity, because they spent a week at a camp I was directing.

Never once did I consider the fact that these justifiably irate parents could have shut the camp down faster than I could blink. Never did the risk occur to me that the parents of these dehydrated and broken-wrist campers could have chosen to spread the word throughout our community to avoid our camp like the plague. Never did I consider the risk that the children who were placed in my care could be in danger of suffering long-lasting harm or physical pain because of the activities I had planned for them. "*What was I thinking?*"

Little did I know that less than a few weeks into my stint as a young and naïve camp director, I was learning a lesson that has remained with me for more than forty years in leadership. In my first few days as a young leader, I came face to face with a trait that is seldom acknowledged yet always present in the life of every leader. And what I've learned over the years is that this trait is so critical that it may just be *the* hidden ingredient that sets individuals and leaders apart.

What I learned in those "*What was I thinking?*" moments was this: life is not without risk. And what has become all too apparent to me is that the ability to make good decisions and to take wise risks is the hidden ingredient that sets a leader apart. In order to reach our full potential in life we must face and take risks. But taking foolish risks can be destructive.

> The ability to make good decisions and to take wise risks is the hidden ingredient that sets a leader apart.

As a young leader I quickly learned that becoming too comfortable with risks (or even being oblivious to them) leaves the very people we hope to lead with the sense that we are foolish—maybe even dangerous. And I've yet to find many people who are out searching to find and to follow a foolish, dangerous leader.

So why was I struggling so much at managing risks? What was causing me to take foolish risks? What was off in my risk-taking calculations?

What's curious is that I have always considered myself to be risk-averse. I have no desire to take unnecessary chances. I've never jumped out of an airplane, nor do I have any desire to do so. As a kid at the roller rink, I never risked rejection by asking a girl to skate with me during "couples-only skate." I have never given in to silly dares or challenges. Why would I? Why would I go out of my way to experience pain, harm, or loss?

Thus, here's the challenge—without risks, we won't rise or make forward progress; but with risk, we might be setting ourselves up to fail. *Forward movement requires both a willingness and ability to take risks.* If we risk too little, we limit the potential of the very thing we are leading and attempting to move forward. But at the same time, as we take risks, we expose ourselves to situational factors than can lead to catastrophic failure.

And here lies the tension for every one of us who make decisions and with every decision we face. *How do I manage risk wisely?*

• • •

On February 4, 2018, coach Doug Pederson and the Philadelphia Eagles found themselves in uncharted territory. Never before had the Eagles been so close to winning so much. In the closing moments of the second quarter of Super Bowl LII, the Eagles were facing a fourth-and-goal. That's when coach Pederson called a play that many have labeled one of the gutsiest play-calls in Super Bowl history.

As risky as it was, the play known as the Philly Special (also known as Philly Philly) was successful, and resulted in a touchdown which led to a victory—the Eagles' first ever Super Bowl win.

NFL Films described it as "a play that the Eagles had never called before, run on 4th down by an undrafted rookie running back pitching the football to a third-string tight-end who had never attempted an NFL pass before, throwing to a backup quarterback who had never caught an NFL (or college) pass before, pulled off on the biggest stage for football." Talk about taking a risk![1]

Life is not without risk. And the ability to manage risk and to know how to take calculated risks is the hidden ingredient that sets a leader and football teams apart.

• • •

For twelve years I had worked on the staff of a large church in the suburbs of Dallas. The church was stable and growing, and a great environment for me to develop and learn. Of course, being in Dallas meant I could read or listen to reports about my beloved Dallas Cowboys 24/7. And the fact that my dad was the senior pastor of this church afforded my wife Ruth and me the opportunity to spend lots of time with extended family. It was the ideal situation.

Until it wasn't. A discontent began to stir inside me. I felt this growing desire for change and to lead on my own. So we began exploring other churches, speaking to them about leadership opportunities.

And we talked to God. We felt we were being very generous with God. We said, "We'll go anywhere you lead us, God . . . anywhere, that is, as long as it's in Texas." A bit closed-minded you might think, but if you weren't born or raised in Texas, then you might not understand that from the day you are born, you are taught never to leave the state of Texas. Why would you? What could be better than Texas? The sense of pride that comes from being a native Texan is like none other.

Embedded in our decision to stay in Texas was that, at this exact same time, Ruth and I were waiting for the opportunity to adopt our second child. The agency that placed our first child with us (a smiley baby boy with the biggest brown eyes) had the practice of placing a second baby in the home of that same adoptive family . . . as long as that family remained in Texas. The possibility of moving away from Texas carried with it great risks for our family—risks we were not ready to bear.

For two years we looked and waited for the right church. We spoke with more than thirty churches. None seemed to be the right fit. It wasn't until after a great deal of consternation and prayer that we took a risk and opened up our search—and our hearts—and truly allowed God to lead us wherever he pleased.

Exactly one month after taking that risk, God blessed us with our second adoption (an adorable baby girl). Less than two months later, we were contacted by a church in Pennsylvania. Six months later, facing the biggest decision of my professional career, Ruth and I decided to follow God, pull up our Texas roots and move to Pennsylvania—or as our Texas friends would say, the Rust Belt. "Why would you possibly want to move away from Texas? Why, especially, would you want to move to the Rust Belt?"

We took a giant risk and followed God. Truth be told, our next five years with this little church were rough. Again and again I found myself asking the question, "*What was I thinking?*" Why had I decided to move our family from a loving and accepting church full of friends and family in Dallas into what felt like a hostile environment in the Northeast?

Six months into the position, our first Elder Board chairman resigned—the same chairman who had recruited me from Texas. Mid-meeting, he stood up and announced to the rest of the board members, "You don't need *me* anymore; you have David." And as he stood, he ceremoniously removed from his key chain the key to the church building, slapped it on the conference room table and walked out the door.

"What was I thinking?" was the question ringing through my head.

Twelve months later, our next Elder Board Chairman did the same exact thing. Mid-meeting he stood, ceremoniously removed from his key chain the key to the church, and walked out the door. (It was then that I realized that everyone in a small church has a key to the church building!) *"What was I thinking?"*

In those first five years, congregational meetings were well attended. Why wouldn't they be? They were always full of fireworks! In spite of our struggles, the church had grown to more than 300 people, and we were discussing the opportunity of hiring our first additional staff member, a worship leader from Nebraska. The room was full and the tension was high when the first man stood and asked, "Why would we hire anybody? Nobody can work with David." A second man stood and said, "We've already got a cowboy from Texas, why do we need to hire a farmer from Nebraska?"

"What was I thinking?"

Then things began to click. Somewhere along the way, between our fifth of sixth year, we stopped talking about what kind of church God wanted us to be, and we started *being* the church God wanted us to be. And today, what was formerly known as Lancaster County Bible Church but is now LCBC Church (Lives Changed By Christ), has grown from 150 people to 20,000 people, spread across central and eastern Pennsylvania in nineteen locations.

Here's what's fun: thirty-something years later, people are now asking us that same question, but with a twist. They ask Ruth and me the same question that has rung in our ears countless times. They asked this same question because risks are not one-dimensional. Risks are two-sided. Risks involve both threats and opportunities. So now when they ask the question, *"What were you thinking?"* they asked it with a twist. Now they ask, "When you moved from Texas to Pennsylvania, did you ever dream this would happen? Did you ever dream so many lives would be changed by Christ when you first came? What were you thinking?"

• • •

Without risks, we won't rise or make forward progress, but with risk, we are setting ourselves up to potentially fail.

King Solomon said it this way: "Farmers who wait for perfect weather never plant. If they watch every cloud, they never harvest" (Eccles. 11:4).

Life is not without risk. And the ability to manage risk and to know how to take calculated risks, is the hidden ingredient that sets a leader apart.

CHAPTER 2

THE BOY WHO JUMPED

A six-year-old boy and his family were spending the week at his grandparents' home that summer. His mother's family was Italian, so the house was always filled with activity, loud conversation, laughter, and the aroma of something delicious in the kitchen. His closest siblings, an older sister and younger brother, sat with him on the creaky porch glider, kicking their feet in unison in an attempt to make *sitting* feel more like *fun*. It worked—at least for a little while. But then boredom set in.

The porch was constructed of yellow brick with a gray wooden floor. Its walls were about a foot thick, wide enough on top for a child to perch. The side wall rose about 5 to 6 feet above the ground, where a concrete walkway ran between the grandparents' home and the neighbors'. Looking for a little more excitement, the three children squatted atop the wall, like catchers in the bullpen, daring one another to jump. Surely that would be more thrilling than the porch glider! And besides, anyone who might consider porch-jumping a bad idea was sitting in the house completely unaware of the opportunity facing the family's three youngest.

The little boy thought, *Who's going to stop me? This will be great!* With one last glance at his sister and brother, he jumped.

Something wasn't quite right about the landing, but the boy stood up, brushed himself off, and turned to look up at his siblings. His sister placed a hand over her mouth, pointed at the blood that was now streaming down the boy's face, and let out a scream. As the boy made his way to the front of the porch and up the stairs, those inside had heard the screams and ran out to investigate.

There was no car, nor any licensed drivers home at the time. Grandma picked up the boy and walked out on the lawn yelling, "Does anybody have a car?!" The boy's mother was by their side trying to compose herself. A few doors down, a young soldier on leave bolted out of his parents' home and offered a ride to the hospital. The soldier honked his horn and pointed to the bloodied child as he barreled through red lights and stop signs.

In the end, the boy received twelve stitches to his forehead, earning him the nickname "Frankenstein" when he returned to school a few weeks later. For the next decade or so, his siblings blamed him for ruining their summer vacation. You see, after his little mishap, no one else was allowed to do anything dangerous (a.k.a., "fun") for the remainder of the week. Even the glider was off limits!

That little boy was me (Rob), and the porch jump is one of my earliest memories of a conscious risk assessment. I won't bore you with more tales of the foolish risks I took in the years that followed, nor of the opportunities I missed because my own fears held me back. But like you, I suppose, I can readily identify a dozen or so key decisions in my life (follow Christ; sell a motorcycle; propose to my wife; change careers; start a business; back out of a real estate deal), where I chose to risk or not to risk, that have had a profound impact on who I am and what I do today.

• • •

I like to think that I learn from experience, but sometimes I do the same foolish thing several times before anything resembling *learning* sets in. Some of the lessons really have no moral implications, like the countless times I've tried to save a few bucks by fixing something myself when I would have done less damage to my house or my body had I called a qualified electrician or plumber.

But much of my learning has come through *moral* failings—from times when I overestimated my character, willpower, or self-control as I waded into damaging choices. I have realized how weak and vulnerable I truly am to moral failing—to drifting from God—which has given me deeper appreciation for his grace in forgiving my sins. Though I have gained wisdom and shed some impulsivity with age, old flaws occasionally resurface, and new ones emerge.

Today, a good portion of my work involves coaching leaders and entrepreneurs one-on-one. Many of these individuals are high capacity, C-level executives and business owners from a wide range of industries. Some run small enterprises, and others fairly large ones. Around 10–15 percent of my work is with churches, ministries, or secular nonprofits.

I see what high-achievers go through—the good and bad, the risks and rewards. I experience them directly and also through the eyes of those who surround them—their boards, bosses, peers, and subordinates. I have great and genuine admiration for these people. I find most to be of exceptional character. They understand the weight of responsibility on their shoulders, and most truly strive to make the world a better place.

As a psychologist, I always want to know the backstory of the leaders I work with. How have circumstances, experiences, and choices shaped the person sitting across the table from me? Who were the key influencers in their lives? Were there any critical turning points or defining moments impacting their view of the world or of themselves?

To be clear, I am not one to argue that one's past experiences *determine* his or her future, but I would say that each of us is, to *some* extent, a product of our experiences. For example, I grew up with five older sisters (and a younger brother). As a result, I was delivered to my wife, Marita, already well-trained to put the toilet seat down after each use. She credits my sisters for that. I also reflect on the fact that the two most influential mentors in my career were women, and I can't help but attribute that, at least in part, to having sisters I looked up to.

So in hearing these backstories, two things I've noticed about leaders and entrepreneurs is that they have a knack for seeing opportunities that others simply do not or cannot see, and they are willing to risk where others play it safe.

One quits a secure job for the prospect of building a company from scratch, knowing that most companies fail within a few years. Another risks costly expansion of facilities to prepare for growth that may or may not come. And another leaves behind a twenty-year high-paying career so she can start a ministry. Most would not describe themselves as particularly creative. Instead, they say things like, "I just put two and two together," or "It just seemed to make sense to me."

While some describe themselves as risk-takers, most say they take only *calculated* risks—that they carefully evaluate choices before proceeding, and that for every risk they've embraced, there were several others they considered but declined. With "successful" people, we readily see their achievements, but we may not be aware of their failed ventures and setbacks—times when they risked, failed, learned, and moved on, or when they persisted far beyond the point where most others would have given up.

Unfortunately, notoriety and influence are usually accompanied by a host of opportunities and pressures that potentially lead to dark places. Pride, greed, lust, and abuses of power have marred the legacies of countless men and women of influence who once seemed so virtuous. Their proclivity for risk was a key ingredient to their initial success but became their Achilles' heel.

We all have blind spots—shortcomings in character or counterproductive behaviors that we cannot see in ourselves but are often evident to those around us. When we fail, we usually do not fall alone. We often drag others along and mar whatever accomplishments we may have previously achieved. How is it, I've often wondered, that genuinely good and seemingly wise people can make such bone-headed choices and risk losing their reputations and all they've achieved? And what's the secret for those who manage to avoid such trappings?

It may seem we are asking, "How can a person take risks safely?" That's kind of a silly question—if risks were safe, they really wouldn't be risks at all. To reach our full potential, we must be willing to risk failure—and we should *expect* to fail *sometimes*. But there is a big difference between risking and failing to achieve a challenging goal versus risking and tarnishing one's legacy. Our aim is to encourage the former and guard against the latter. If we must be willing to take risks in order to fulfill our God-given potential, how can we do so *safely enough* to avoid self-destruction?

CHAPTER 3

THE DANGER OF PLAYING IT SAFE

Known for his aggressive driving style, he earned the nickname, "The Intimidator." NASCAR driver Dale Earnhardt Sr. chose to embrace risk, and as a result he is regarded as one of the greatest drivers in NASCAR history. But in 2001, Dale Sr. died in a violent crash at the Daytona 500.

Because of his willingness to chase risks, Dale Earnhardt Sr. won seventy-six races. But because of his willingness to chase risks, Dale Earnhardt Sr. also died at the age of forty-nine while in third place on the final lap of the 2001 Daytona 500. Dale left behind four children and millions of adoring fans.

Months later, a tribute to Dale Earnhardt Sr. was held at the Waldorf-Astoria Hotel in New York City. On massive screens, photo after photo of Earnhardt displayed win and win after win, all because he was willing to chase risks.

While these photos of Dale Earnhardt's life and career were on display, country singing legend Garth Brooks sang the words to his iconic song, "The Dance." There wasn't a dry eye in the house as Garth sang the words to his song that stated it so well: *"I could have missed the pain, But I'd have had to miss the dance."* Bottom line, yes, Dale Earnhardt Sr. might still be alive had he not pursued so many risks on the racetrack. But if he had played it safe, the legend never would have existed.

• • •

One day, Jesus told a story about risks. In this story that is recorded in the biblical book of Matthew, a wealthy man puts his riches into the hands of three individuals. Each of the three received a portion of the rich man's wealth based on their ability to handle risk wisely. With his money now in the hands of three individuals, the rich man heads out of town for a long trip.

When the rich man returns home, he quickly calls the three individuals together in order for them to give an account of his money. The first two individuals step forward and declare that because they took risks on some wise investments, the rich man's money has now been doubled. Which is extraordinary.

The rich man responds with praise and celebration and extends even more responsibilities to the two who managed the risks so wisely. "Well done, my good and faithful servant," the master said to the two. "You have been faithful in handling this small amount, so now I will give you many more responsibilities. Let's celebrate together!" (Matt. 25:21).

But the third individual took a dramatically different approach. Rather than risking the loss of the rich man's money through investments, he eliminated all risks by simply burying the money in the ground. Why take a risk on losing his money? "I was afraid I would lose your money, so I hid it in the earth. Look, here is your money back" (v. 25).

To which the rich man responds (and we paraphrase), *"What were you thinking?"*

"What was I thinking? I'll tell you what I was thinking. I was thinking you are a harsh man. I was thinking I don't want to risk losing what is yours. I was thinking I'll play it safe and do nothing. I was thinking it's not worth the risk." All seemingly logical explanations from the third individual.

Logical? Maybe. Acceptable? Apparently not. *"You wicked and lazy person! At the very least you could have put my money in the bank and let it draw interest."* There was no praise from the rich man. There was no celebration. Instead, all future responsibility was removed and given to the two who were willing to take risks.

Jesus ends his story with this: "To those who use well what they are given, even more will be given, and they will have an abundance. But from those who do nothing, even what little they have will be taken away" (v. 29).

Clearly, Jesus is saying you and I are expected to do something with the talents and resources God has given us. And this involves taking risks. Those who play it safe rarely break away from a life of mediocrity—instead, they bury their talents in the sand and fail to multiply what has been entrusted to their care.

• • •

What motivated Dale Earnhardt Sr. to risk driving around an oval track at 200 mph, while the rest of us are content to set the cruise control at 7 mph above the speed limit on the interstate? What caused two individuals to take risks in order to multiply their master's funds while a third chose to play it safe and take no risks at all?

What causes a leader to risk pushing his team forward when others are satisfied with the status quo? What makes a pastor choose to take risks that will move his congregation further and faster? Why is one person risk-averse and another risk-tolerant?

Is it just a matter of personality? Are some people simply more prone to risk-taking than others and thus destined to success—or epic failure? And does success only come to those who have a sense of adventure and who want to try new things? Is victory reserved only for those who are quick to make decisions and more accepting of failure (or even death) than others?

Is it possible for those of us who are more cautious by nature to learn to take risks? And what about those of us who are willing to wait for proven and predictable outcomes, who tend to stick with time-tested practices? What's in store for those of us who find ourselves somewhat skeptical of ever achieving the rewards often associated with taking risks? What about those of us who have not been fortunate enough to be born with good risk-taking gut instincts?

After years of watching and working with all types of leaders with all types of personalities in a variety of church and business settings, we believe that it is possible for all people to develop the skill of making good decisions and taking wise risks. And this is good news, because if we have any hope of living our lives to the fullest, we must learn to embrace risks. Our ability to manage risks well will determine whether or not we break away from a life of mediocrity.

> We believe that it is possible for all people to develop the skill of making good decisions and taking wise risks.

When it comes to taking risks, there is a danger in choosing to play it too safe. Yes, some will choose to dance too close to the edge, but it is our observation that most leaders are prone to playing it too safe. Therefore, it is critical for all leaders to develop the skills necessary to make good decisions and take wise risks.

● ● ●

In my early years as a pastor, I (David) was heavily influenced by Dr. John Maxwell. Every month I looked forward to receiving in the mail John's latest leadership lessons. It was the early '90s—so think cassette tapes. Because my only cassette player was in my car, I listened to John wherever I went.

Which meant my family had to listen to John wherever we went. Before heading out on vacations I would grab a handful of John Maxwell cassettes, and off we would go. To which my family would ask, "Do we have to take John on vacation with us again? Can't we just leave John at home this one time?"

One of my favorite John Maxwell leadership lessons revolves around the fact that every leader is given a certain number of leadership coins to carry in their pockets to use and risk wisely while leading. With each positive decision that a leader makes, they in turn receive more leadership coins to work with. Every negative decision made results in the loss of coins. As long as a leader has coins in their pocket, they are allowed to lead. But once you run out of leadership coins and your pockets are empty, your leadership journey is done.

It is extremely important to know how many leadership coins we have in our pockets at all times. The more coins we have in our pockets, the more risks we can take. The fewer the coins, the more cautious we must be. The bigger the risk, the more leadership coins are required. The smaller the risk, the fewer coins are required.

Thus, young leaders must be wise and take calculated risks that will result in more leadership coins being deposited in their pockets. Start with small decisions that lead to small victories that bring more coins. The more coins we have from past successes, the more we are willing to take risks in the future. The fewer leadership coins in our possession, the more risk-averse we become.

But there is danger in playing it too safe. Playing it safe by standing still and taking no risk is not a safer option. While standing still, we gain no new leadership coins. Sometimes it is wise to take a momentary pause in the action to regroup and replenish our strength. But churches and organizations are like people: we are either moving forward, or we are falling back and losing ground. To acquire more coins, we must learn to manage risks wisely.

• • •

I (David) was thirty-four years old when we moved from Texas to Pennsylvania to pastor and lead the 150 people who were a part of what was then known as Lancaster County Bible Church. The year was 1991, and we were informed by those in the community that the best way to do church in Lancaster County was to wear suits and ties, sing only to an organ and piano, preach standing behind a large pulpit, speak in a way that demonstrates a vast knowledge of Scripture, and above all else, cater only to those already in the church. "That's just how church is done in Lancaster County! After all, this is not Texas!"

Being young (and somewhat naïve), I was willing to embrace risks in order to move our small church forward. With only a few leadership coins in my pockets, we first did away with the large and rather imposing pulpit. To the surprise of many and to the dismay of some, we quickly discovered that God's Word could still penetrate the hearts of listeners even without a monstrosity of a pulpit.

Armed now with a few more leadership coins in my pockets, we gradually began to add a guitar to the organ and piano. Then a second guitar. Then drums. Then the organ sat on the platform unused for over two years until someone finally asked the obvious: "Why do we have that organ sitting on the stage?" To which we responded, "We don't know!" and we gave our organ away to a local college.

As additional leadership coins accumulated in my pockets, we moved from suits and ties to sports coats and ties, to sports coats with no ties, and then to sweaters. For more than two years all the men wore sweaters to church—which was great in the cold of winter but was a killer in the summer heat! Finally, someone said, "Why are we wearing these ugly sweaters?" To which we responded, "We don't know!" So we cast our sweaters aside and began to just dress normal. And jeans and sports shirts became the norm.

But don't make the mistake of thinking these changes came without a price. During my early years at LCBC I often asked myself, "*What was I thinking?*"

I suppose part of what I was thinking was, *Why not? What do I have to lose?* I was young. The church was small. Those most offended already knew Jesus and were already going to heaven. But 85 percent of Lancaster County residents had no church home. Most still needed Jesus. God was big enough to move our little church forward and use us to see more lives changed by Christ. So why not embrace risk?

Early in life, we have less to lose. With less to lose we're more willing to take risks—we don't have that much to lose anyway. But as we get older, as we acquire more, we become more fearful of losing what we have. Because we might lose everything we have worked so hard to achieve, we become fearful of making personal decisions that involve risks. We're tempted to play it safe. To guard what we have.

● ● ●

After delivering the people of Israel from 400 years in slavery, God made an incredible promise to them: he promised them land, land that they could build on and live off of and even own themselves. All that was necessary to possess this land promised by God was simply to take it.

But there were obstacles to taking the land. After exploring it, scouts returned only to report that their promised land was already occupied by others. Yes, the land was fertile, so fertile that two men were required to carry one cluster of grapes. Yes, the land was bountiful—a land flowing with milk and honey. But already inhabiting the land were men much bigger and stronger than the Israelites. Men so strong they would likely devour the Israelites. Men so big that the Israelites felt like grasshoppers in comparison. To take and possess this land that had been promised by God would require extraordinary risk.

Twelve men went out to scout the land. Ten of them were risk-averse. These ten men said, "We can't go up against them! They are stronger than we are!" (Num. 13:31). They couldn't see how they could possibly capture what God had already promised to them. "The land we traveled through and explored will devour anyone who goes to live there," they said (v. 32).

In contrast, two of the twelve scouts had a high tolerance for risks. "Let's go at once to take the land. We can certainly conquer it! . . . Don't be afraid of the people of the land. They are only helpless prey to us! They have no protection, but the LORD is with us! Don't be afraid of them!" (13:30; 14:9). Two men were willing to move forward and take the necessary risks to take control of the land God had promised to them.

But who did the people listen to? Ten leaders convinced the entire nation of Israel to play it safe, and an entire generation of Israelites therefore missed out on the promised land.

Sometimes it is more dangerous to play it safe than to take a risk.

• • •

As leaders, fear can be the enemy of opportunity. Yes, what may lie ahead looks inviting. Yes, moving the organization forward would be great. Yes, more people may be introduced to Jesus. But what if we fail? What if I lose too many leadership coins?

So often, our greatest opportunity may be just on the other side of fear.

• • •

The Eastman Kodak Company was founded in 1888, and over the next century produced and made cameras available to every household in the world. By 1968 Kodak had captured 80 percent of the global market share in the field of photography.

In 1975, Steve Sasson, an electrical engineer at Kodak, invented the digital camera. When Steve told his bosses at Kodak about his invention, their response was basically, "That's cute, but don't tell anyone about it." Fearful that this new technology would cut into their profitable sales of things such as film and printing sheets, Kodak flat-out rejected this new digital world.

Because Kodak ignored this new technology and failed to adapt to the changing market dynamics, soon a Japanese company by the name of "Fuji Films" started the production and sales of digital cameras, leaving Kodak behind in the race. For the next ten years Kodak tried to convince people that film cameras were better than digital cameras. Kodak was just sure that people loved the touch and feel of a printed image over viewing an image captured on a digital camera. By the time Kodak understood their mistakes and started the sales and production of digital cameras, it was too late. By 2012, Kodak filed for bankruptcy. There is a danger in playing it safe.

• • •

Thirty-eight years after the people of Israel passed on their first opportunity to enter the land that God had promised to give them, God presented them with a second opportunity. Both times, the risks were immense. As the people stood before the Jordan River, God said it was time to enter their new land, land that spread for miles and miles across the Jordan River.

Standing before the dividing line between the past and the future, Joshua, one of only two people remaining who had ever seen the beauty of this rich and fertile land, admonished the people to be strong and very courageous and trust in their mighty God as they took their new land.

The Jordan River, overflowing its banks and with a strong and rapid current due to the melting winter snows of Mount Hermon in the north, seemed impossible to cross. Coupled with the knowledge that large and menacing troops of enemies were waiting on the other side, not surprisingly, the people of Israel began to lose heart. The risks of stepping into the Jordan River were great.

But God had promised that as soon as their feet touched the water, the flow of the river would be cut off upstream, and the water would stand up like a wall.

So, the people left their camp and moved to the water's edge. At Joshua's direction, they embraced the risks and stepped into the water. The Bible tell us that as soon as their feet touched the water, sure enough, the water above that point began backing up a great distance away until the riverbed was dry. Then all the people crossed over the river.

This time, the people leaned into the risks. Instead of shying away because of their fears, they stepped into a new land—a new land that was fertile and rich, flowing with milk and honey. And they experienced firsthand, again and again, the might and greatness of God and of his provision for his people.

• • •

Learning to manage risks well does not mean we are relegated to only playing it safe. Rather, it is our belief that good decision-making and wise risk-taking are skills that can be broken down and refined until a leader can learn to excel while still taking risks.

In the pages that follow, we will introduce a model that leads to good decisions and wise risk-taking. A model that will help you take more calculated risks as you pursue the future God has for your life. A model that can guide your staff and your team toward better decisions.

Our model presumes we are already taking certain basic steps when exploring risks. These steps include searching Scripture for direction as well as talking and listening to God and being open to the nudging of God's Spirit. But beyond a sense of God's leading or nudges, we believe it is possible to quantify those gut feelings which in turn allows us to respond to risks in a Spirit-led and calculated fashion.

And as we learn together to manage risks well, may we each hear the Master say, "Well done, my good and faithful servant. You have been faithful in handling this small amount, so now I will give you many more responsibilities. Let's celebrate together!"

PART 2

CHAPTER 4

THE MODEL

Human beings operate in a constant state of decision-making. As we mentioned earlier, in any given day, we make thousands upon thousands of decisions.

For most of these, we don't waste much energy worrying about what to do, or wondering if we made the right decision. But every decision produces some consequence. So, this morning, had I (Rob) deviated by choosing to shut my eyes rather than placing my feet on the floor when my alarm sounded, my day would have turned out quite differently than it did.

Many of the decisions we make have a *near-certain outcome*: tying my shoe will almost certainly secure it to my foot; inserting my contact lenses will enable me to see clearly; wearing a coat will keep me warmer than not wearing one. Anyone who shares my passion for hunting may recognize these near-certain outcome decisions as well: carrying my deer rifle will ensure I see only turkeys; carrying my shotgun will ensure I see only deer; not packing rain gear will bring rain.

Our model for making good decisions is not so concerned with the types of decisions that come with near-certain outcomes. Rather, we're more interested in that subset of decisions involving an element of *risk*—decisions that bring meaningful exposure to the chance of injury or loss. And we believe it is possible to break down these decisions involving risks in a way that allows us to make wise and calculated decisions about those risks.

• • •

Dawson Childers had a comfortable life. His parents owned a local construction company that was started by Dawson's grandfather in 1973. The two had purchased this rather small operation in the mid-1980s and grew it into a thriving business that provided nicely for the family. Dawson had grown up around the business, washing trucks every Saturday afternoon as a young child, and working with the crews in the field each summer as he progressed through high school and college. He never enjoyed the fieldwork, however, so after earning a college degree, he took a position in the company's IT department.

His older sister and brother also worked in the family business, in project management and estimating units, respectively. Dawson's parents dreamed of one day transitioning the business to their three children who would own and lead it together, thus building upon the family legacy. His siblings enjoyed their work and thrived in their roles. Dawson *performed* well, but was unable to muster much enthusiasm about the prospect of spending the next several decades with the company, despite the economic security it would most certainly bring.

Dawson's family had always been active in their local church and generous in their contributions to both ministries and other charitable organizations. Dawson enjoyed ministry work, and though he had no particular ambitions to lead, would typically find himself placed "in charge" in nearly every area he volunteered. As he thought back, Dawson realized this had been the case since his high school participation in youth group, through his role as president of the campus ministry in college, and now in several service and teaching involvements as an adult. He had even been tapped to preach on multiple occasions when the lead pastor was away, after which there would invariably come encouraging, half-joking remarks like, "Pastor Jim better watch his back—you're pretty good." "Are you sure you're in the right field? That sermon turned out much better than that new office complex your family just built," and the like.

Truth is, after working the last six years in the family business and now being married with a second child on the way, Dawson himself began to wonder if he was in the right field. In one sense, he felt pulled toward vocational ministry. But the prospect of leaving the family business, forfeiting his opportunity to gain shared ownership of a valuable enterprise, and retooling for a new career that brings low pay, unusual hours, and a high failure rate, all seemed a bit daunting.

The safer bet would be to stay put. Safer and more predictable, but one that had thus far brought only limited fulfillment. Pursuing a career in ministry seemed *potentially* and perhaps *likely* more fulfilling to Dawson, but there were no guarantees.

Dawson found himself at a fork in the road. Should he stay with the family business or pursue a career in ministry? Neither choice was *morally* superior to the other—just different in terms of what he would be placing at risk.

BIG DECISION #1

As you might have guessed, Dawson became "Pastor Dawson." In this instance, we would argue that Dawson's choice displayed the kind of risk initiative that characterizes "breakaway" leaders—that inclination to step forward in faith which tends to produce extraordinary impact. He chose to place *potential* over *comfort*.

We are not suggesting it is inherently better to choose careers in ministry over careers in business. For some people, the step of faith—the choice with potential for extraordinary impact— might lead them *from* vocational ministry *to* the marketplace. In fact, one of us (David) left an early career in business for ministry, and the other (Rob) left a mid-career position in ministry for one in the marketplace.

So Dawson spent the next four years accruing the skills, knowledge, and experience he would need to prepare himself to pastor a small church. An offer came from Bigler Community Church (hereafter referred to as "BCC" since every good church needs a memorable acronym), located in a rural setting about 600 miles away from family. Dawson and his wife, Beth, along with now three young children, had never lived far from their hometown, but off they went.

If there was a single decision Dawson had been sure of, it was marrying Beth. Beth consistently voiced support for Dawson's career and felt every bit as called to ministry as he had. But Dawson knew that she also felt isolated and that it would take time to build new friendships. Beth was sacrificing a lot for him and, as the new pastor's wife, already sensed the pressure of watchful eyes to be the exemplary spouse, mother, and ministry partner.

BCC was a new church of about 125 people, with three different elders sharing the pastoring duties until Dawson came on board as its first full-time pastor. In time, the church grew significantly under Dawson's leadership. To be sure, there were setbacks along the way, but with a few battle scars and the passage of another four years, BCC was approaching 350 in weekly attendance, with three paid staff.

Dawson was working harder than ever but took great satisfaction in seeing God grow the church and extend its reach. It was common for him to burn the candle on both ends, scheduling breakfast meetings with key volunteers and community influencers, yet also feeling a need to be visible at all church activities, many of which occurred in the evenings. As a result, he often left home before Beth and the children were up and sometimes was kept away until after his kids were asleep.

He tried to take off each Tuesday, but pastoral "emergencies" sometimes disrupted that plan, and Saturdays were occasionally consumed by weddings and more sermon prep. He commonly worked more than sixty hours a week and continued to press ahead despite the obvious strain. It was both tiring and exhilarating, and Dawson was grateful to be at the center of what seemed so obviously a "work of God."

BIG DECISION #2

To hear Dawson describe the situation, he never really thought of it as a conscious decision. He characterized it more as a "drifting" of sorts.

Lindsay Whitcomb, who was about Dawson's age, volunteered two days each week at the church office, providing administrative support to the pastors, scheduling volunteers, and handling a variety of special projects. As a general rule, the church did not permit two persons of opposite sex to work in the office unless there was at least one other person present. There was good chemistry between the pastors and Lindsay, who proved herself smart, capable, and energetic. Everyone liked having her around, as she had a knack for lifting the mood in any room she entered.

Dawson said of this drifting,

> I found myself looking forward to seeing
> Lindsay come into the office each day. She had
> a great smile, laughed at my jokes, and was
> always helpful. It was all innocent, but I have to
> admit that it felt good to have someone paying
> that kind of attention to me. And with Beth so
> wrapped up in the kids' activities, I was no lon-
> ger getting much of that from her. It's not that
> things were bad between Beth and me. We were
> both just too busy and tired all the time to really
> be there for each other.
>
> It didn't really hit me until last Thursday.
> The others had gone home, so it was just
> Lindsay and me left at the office. I was working
> on my sermon and wanted her opinion on how
> I was planning to phrase something, so I called
> her in to look at my computer screen. She leaned
> a little close. I felt the tips of her hair brush my
> neck, and I noticed how nice she smelled. And
> then she reached over me to type a correction
> on the keyboard.
>
> I felt myself flush with a weird mix of
> excitement and fear, like a sixteen-year-old on
> his first date, mustering the courage to put his
> arm around his date in the movie theater. I

think I said something awkwardly flirty, and then she shot back with a similar remark.

I knew I was about to cross a line. But then I thought of Beth. The shame and embarrassment hit me like a ton of bricks. I must have turned beet red. I could tell Lindsay felt it too. She apologized for making me uncomfortable. I lied and said it was no big deal. I thanked her for helping me with my sermon, and then she left. And that was it.

I thought to myself, *How could I even go there? I'm not that kind of person.* Yet there I was. Again, I thought of Beth and the kids. And I suddenly realized just how close I'd come to throwing away what I thought was a good marriage, losing my job, destroying any credibility I had in challenging others to follow Christ, and essentially obliterating my life's work. And that's to say nothing of Lindsay's husband and family. *"What was I thinking?!"*

• • •

Dawson is a fictional character. But you know Dawson Childers. He's like you. He's like me. He's like someone you work with. Over our years of experience interacting with leaders in business and ministry settings, we have seen stories very similar to Dawson's play out many times. Dawson's account is the only fictional one you'll find in this book. The other stories we put forth are constructed from actual situations that we have encountered or become aware of in the course of our work. We have typically disguised or altered key elements of each story so as to prevent identification of the persons involved.

So what might Dawson's story tell us about the way people choose to risk or not risk? Dawson was making thousands of decisions each day, but for the sake of learning to make good decisions and to take wise risks, we've pulled out two of his biggest decisions.

We have so far argued that individuals who live life to its fullest are neither reckless nor timid—that God has given each of us a sphere of influence in which to make good decisions and a positive difference. We have encouraged you to venture beyond what may be comfortable and to take healthy risks, yet cautioned against recklessness.

> God has given each of us a sphere of influence in which to make good decisions and a positive difference.

A life well-lived and pleasing to God is one characterized by both faith—which by its nature requires risk—and wise restraint. If you are too risk-averse, you may be settling for a ho-hum existence—producing a degree of impact that falls short of what it might have been. As we asked earlier, isn't that a key lesson of the parable of the three servants (Matt. 25:14–30)?

And yet if you risk recklessly (as Dawson nearly did), then you may gravely tarnish or even destroy your reputation and nullify your life's work. When Christians do that, the damage is compounded. As we are told in 2 Corinthians 5:20, we should see ourselves as "ambassadors" of Christ—as representatives of Jesus to the world around us. In that sense, our reckless behavior can blemish the reputation of Christ. We become a source of repulsion *from* Christ rather than a source of attraction *to* him.

Therefore, we have developed a model that aims to help us make better and calculated decisions so we can lead and live with confidence. We believe that for any decision where risk is involved, we will invariably encounter four distinct propositions—four propositions to risk. These four propositions invite us either to enter the risk before us or to back away from that risk. How we progress through the four propositions will ultimately determine whether we choose to initiate or avoid the risk at hand.

What is important to understand is that these four propositions of risks come at us whether we want them or not. They simply present themselves automatically and cannot be avoided. Thus, in order to make good decisions and take wise risks, we must be aware of them and consciously deal with them.

These four propositions are:

1. What would you like?
2. What is available?

3. Can you make it happen?
4. What might result?

• • •

These four propositions routinely figure into any choice we face to initiate or avoid risk. They may be dealt with reflexively or reflectively, or anywhere in between, but the four propositions invariably bear upon our final choice and should be taken into account when considering taking a risk. The dynamic interplay of these four propositions will determine whether we choose to take a chance in any given set of circumstances. We briefly introduce our model here and will flesh it out in detail in the chapters that follow.

What would you like?

The first proposition is about **desire**. Desire encompasses our wants and cravings. *What do I want in this situation? What do I want out of life?* At its best, desire fuels healthy ambition and focus. It produces go-getters and high-achievers. Desire can lead to exceptional performance in school, sports, or work and can motivate us toward financial security, generosity, good parenting, and spiritual maturity.

But even the most virtuous among us are susceptible to sinful desires. If we're not careful, this dark side of desire leaves us lacking contentment for what God has given us and prone to chasing the wrong things.

What is available?

The second proposition presents **opportunity**. Opportunity is about the *circumstances* that create potential to advance our desires, or the *array of options* available for doing so. For example, a financial blessing that comes in the form of an unexpected tax refund enables a caring parent to afford the tutoring she so desires for her struggling child. Even constraints, like imprisonment, financial loss, or a failed marriage, are part of the opportunity proposition.

Of course, not all opportunity leads to good. A moment of freedom from the eyes of a watchful parent affords opportunity for a child to chase a ball into a busy street. Long hours spent alone with an attractive coworker can lead to marital infidelity, as we saw in Dawson and Lindsay's case. Available credit can bring problematic spending and crushing debt.

Opportunity follows desire, for we can only take advantage of conditions to advance an objective, or generate options for doing so, insofar as we know what that objective might be.

Can you make it happen?

The third proposition concerns **power**. Power is a person's capacity to make a difference—to affect the world in some measurable way. Most people underestimate their power. Many of us with limited financial resources or relatively low-ranking positions at work may actually possess a great deal of power in the home—power that derives from our physical size or strength.

How that power is used as a parent, for example, can be the difference between a home characterized by security or abuse. We will describe how virtuous behavior naturally increases one's power and how virtuous *use* of power can bring about tremendous good.

But there's a catch: power is always seductive and can lead to impaired empathy, self-centeredness, impulsivity, and a host of other counterproductive tendencies. What starts as healthy influence can easily lapse into unhealthy control or even abuse.

What might result?

The fourth proposition involves **expectations**—the anticipated possible outcomes should we choose to act. *What do I expect in this situation? What do I expect out of life?* If we expect an action to produce a desirable result, then we are likely to proceed. And if we expect an unpleasant result, we are likely to halt. Action-oriented people tend to be realistic optimists. They generally expect their efforts to succeed, after which they can envision and conquer the next hill, and the one after that.

Because they are accustomed to success, they expect it to continue. But this can lead them to underestimate the likelihood of a bad outcome to any behavior they may be contemplating. When we think we're immune to getting caught, causing pain, or experiencing loss, we tend to behave foolishly—to do things that end careers, traumatize others, and destroy legacies.

• • •

The diagram below encapsulates our model:

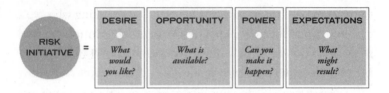

We would like to think our simple model is pretty dope. (As cool and hip as we like to think we are, we had to look up the term *dope* on Dictionary.com to make sure we're using it correctly here. The 13th listed meaning of the word described it as a slang term meaning "great" or "excellent." The sample sentence was, "His band is so dope!" Yep, that's what we were aiming for.)

We hope you agree, but whether you end up seeing it as *dope* or *dopey*, you may find the acronym DOPE a useful device to help you remember the four psychological considerations that determine risk initiative: **D**esire, **O**pportunity, **P**ower, and **E**xpectations. Hereafter, we will refer to our model as "The DOPE Model of Risk Initiative" or just, "The DOPE Model."

• • •

In some situations, the propositions come so quickly or subtly that the decision itself can seem almost reflexive or automatic to its maker. For example, if you were sitting by a riverbank and suddenly saw a child fall into the water and start screaming as she got swept up in the current, you might jump in right away to save her. In fact, when we see such incidents on the evening news and the reporter asks the rescuer, "What were you thinking when you decided to put your own life at risk by jumping in to save that little girl?," the response is often something like, "I didn't really have time to think at all. I just jumped in."

Some potential rescuers might instead look for a rope or stick to toss to the child. Others might run along the riverbank shouting instructions to the child, and still others' first impulse might be to attempt to find and alert the child's parents. The decision of the rescuer may or may not produce a successful outcome for the child. In other words, the risk is real.

And each option carries its own *degree* of risk—perhaps even death—to the rescuers themselves. So, with our hypothetical hero on the local news, the four propositions may have unfolded as follows:

RISK ASSESSMENT: DO I RISK SAVING THIS CHILD FROM DROWNING?

What would you like?—To save the child from harm (Desire)

What is available?—It's me or no one (Opportunity)

Can you make it happen?—Yes, I can swim. (Power)

What might result?—She might die if I don't do something right away. (Expectations)

In this instance, the propositions appeared and were acted upon rapidly, perhaps even subconsciously, but our hero had to, at some level, face each of the four propositions before taking action. We simply cannot initiate risk in the absence of a driving force (Desire); some assessment of our circumstances and options available (Opportunity); our capability to exploit those options (Power); and the potential results of our actions (Expectations).

One can easily imagine how a *different bystander* under the same circumstances might confront or process the four propositions differently, leading to an equally rapid but very different decision and different course of action. For instance:

RISK ASSESSMENT: DO I RISK SAVING THIS CHILD FROM DROWNING?

What would you like?—To save the child from harm (Desire)

What is available?—I could jump in, yell for help, or find some way to intercept her downstream. (Opportunity)

Can you make it happen?—I'm a terrible swimmer, but I can yell and run. (Power)

What might result?—If I jump in, we'll probably both drown. If I run downstream as I yell for help, a better solution may appear. (Expectations)

For risk assessments that take more time to develop or unfold, such as decisions to risk a career change, a financial investment, or an extramarital affair, any or all of the four propositions are likely to be handled and experienced in a more conscious or deliberate manner.

Now let's take a brief look at how the four propositions to risk may have played into Dawson's two big decisions.

DAWSON'S RISK ASSESSMENT: SHOULD I RISK CHANGING CAREERS?

What would you like?—More fulfillment in my daily work (Desire)

What is available?—Stay with the family business; pursue a career in ministry; or explore other careers (Opportunity)

Can you make it happen?—Well, no one is stopping me from pursuing ministry. And yes, I can get the education and experience I would need, and can probably find a way to afford it. Realistically, all three options are viable. (Power)

What might result?—If I stay in the family business, I will do well financially but spend the next forty years doing something I dislike. If I pursue a career in ministry, I will spend the next forty years doing something that will likely bring meaning and enjoyment, but it won't pay very well. It is also possible I would do poorly in either career. God will likely be pleased with any choice I make, insofar as I honor his desires as revealed in the Bible. (Expectations)

In this situation, Dawson could take whatever amount of time he deemed necessary to consider carefully each of the four propositions and deliberately calculate whether to risk a career change.

Not so in Dawson's second big decision. The same four invitations were at play, yet the speed (very rapid) and degree of reflection involved (very little) were quite different.

DAWSON'S RISK ASSESSMENT: DO I TAKE THE RISK TO SEDUCE OR NOT SEDUCE?

What would you like?—Sexual gratification; intimacy (Desire)

What is available?—I am alone with an attractive woman who seems interested in me. (Opportunity)

Can you make it happen?—Yes, I can make a move right now. (Power)

What might result?—Sexual gratification; pleasure; no one will know but the two of us. It will be our secret. Oh wait! Making a move right now might also result in rejection, which would be horribly awkward and embarrassing. Or worse yet, we might go through with it and the secret would get out. Or might go through with it and be crippled by guilt. That would hurt my wife and kids and family, and could destroy my marriage and career. (Expectations)

In this second situation, Dawson may have allowed his desires for gratification and intimacy *with Lindsay* to develop over a period of time, perhaps as a matter of fleeting thoughts or fantasies. But once the opportunity arose (*Here's what's available*), the remaining decisions were encountered rapidly, with very little reflection. In this particular instance, Dawson maintained the presence of mind to consider multiple outcomes (*What might result?*), which enabled him to opt against completing the act he was contemplating.

Unfortunately, human nature usually leaves us so narrowly focused on the arrival of the fourth proposition that we seldom consider expected outcomes that might effectively counter the forces of our potentially destructive desires. Whether those desires tilt us toward safety or risk, human beings are prone to justifying our aims and neglecting information that might steer us away from the path we are already leaning toward.

There is much more we could say about this scenario (we have focused on Dawson only, with no consideration of the situation from Lindsay's perspective; we have said nothing about the power dynamic between a boss and his subordinate, nor about some of the counterproductive habits Dawson had developed in the years and months leading up to the incident), but have opted to present it in simple form for the purpose of illustrating the model in action.

You and I face decisions of similar magnitude on a regular basis. Therefore, in the chapters that follow, we examine the DOPE Model and its four propositions more deeply, offering practical considerations for effectively managing each one. We hope this model will help you make decisions and initiate risk in a godly manner that reflects an active approach and is rooted in both faith and prudence.

Mastering the DOPE Model can't guarantee the correct decision in every situation, but it will allow you to advance with a more calculated decision about the risks you are facing.

CHAPTER 5

PROPOSITION 1: "WHAT WOULD YOU LIKE?"

Every risk ever taken had its root in desire.

That's not to say that every action or behavior imaginable is rooted in desire. We all engage in a variety of somewhat controllable yet unintentional behaviors that may have no connection whatsoever to our desires (blinking our eyes, touching our faces, fidgeting) or that might run counter to our desires (passing gas within earshot or nose-shot of others). But any *intentional* behavior, and certainly any choice to initiate risk (where there is exposure to the chance of injury or loss) is, by its nature, driven by desire.

Twenty-five years ago, our original group of 150 people had grown at LCBC Church (Lives Changed By Christ), and we now filled our auditorium to its 400-person capacity. We faced a decision that involved risks. Were we finished with our mission of introducing more people to Jesus, or did we need to add a second Sunday gathering to our schedule?

The risks were plenty. How would we staff a second gathering with the necessary volunteers when we were struggling to staff just one? How would the church culture be affected? Would we still be able to see our friends and connect with others with two gatherings? But because our desire was to introduce more people to Jesus, we chose to embrace the risks.

Right up until our first Sunday with two gatherings, you could cut the tension with a knife! The 9:00 a.m. gathering went off with flying colors. And by 11:00 a.m. we never heard another word about the risks in hosting two Sunday morning gatherings.

Five years later, we had grown to more than 1,200 in attendance each weekend. The growth was both exhilarating and exhausting. To accommodate the growth, we made the decision to go from two weekend gatherings to three on Sunday mornings with one additional gathering on Saturday night.

The staff was wearing thin, and upon delivering my fourth message of the weekend, my mind was shot. Typically I (David) was good remembering names, but by Sunday afternoon I could hardly recall the names of Ruth, my wife, or Justin and Ashleigh, my kids!

Our leadership team was faced with a decision: Are we done introducing more people to Jesus, or do we need to find another way to keep advancing the good news of Jesus? We wanted to keep moving forward, but forward movement meant taking a risk. To this point our growth had been cheap—at least financially. Growth had cost us nothing other than a lot more work and longer hours!

Our desire was to continue to introduce more people to Jesus, which would require building bigger buildings, which would require raising the funds to do so. The risks were daunting. What if we tried and failed? What if people were offended by being asked to give financially, and left the church? What if we built a bigger building and no new people came?

As we took inventory of our desires, we chose to move ahead with taking the risk of raising funds and building a bigger building. Our desire wasn't to build bigger so that our existing church family would be more comfortable. We were building to open seats for more people to meet and connect with Jesus.

The good news is, people weren't offended by being asked to give financially. And they did give. As a result, we exceeded our financial goal, and we grew by 50 percent in weekly attendance. And that new building gave us the space and capacity to continue to grow over the next six years to more than 6,000 people each weekend.

We prefer not to think of what would have been had we not taken that initial risk, had we shrunk back and stayed with only one weekend gathering.

• • •

When making decisions and taking risks, the first of the four propositions concerns our *desires*, our aspirations, needs, and appetites, the things we *want* or *crave*. This proposition comes in the form, *"What would you like?"*

A desire can be for the short-term ("I'd like something to eat") or the long run ("I'd love to retire comfortably"), and may be morally neutral, virtuous, or sinful. So, for example, the desire to eat when hungry might be aimed at providing strength for the body (a virtuous pursuit) or toward gluttony (a sinful excess).

A desire to retire comfortably might be aimed toward faithful stewardship of resources or intent to live without unduly burdening others (virtues), greed (a vice) or perhaps even toward simple comfort or enjoyment (morally neutral). A desire for sexual gratification can be targeted for fulfillment through mutually pleasing exchange in marriage (a virtue), or through a variety of sexual activities that reflect less virtuous (at best) or flagrantly abusive manifestations of one's sex drive.

The apostle Paul speaks to the internal havoc that can be wreaked upon us as we wrestle with our desires:

And I know that nothing good lives in me, that is, in my sinful nature. I want to do what is right, but I can't. I want to do what is good, but I don't. I don't want to do what is wrong, but I do it anyway. But if I do what I don't want to do, I am not really the one doing wrong; it is sin living in me that does it. I have discovered this principle of life—that when I want to do what is right, I inevitably do what is wrong. I love God's law with all my heart. But there is another power within me that is at war with my mind. This power makes me a slave to the sin that is still within me. (Rom. 7:18–23)

Some desires seem inherently good (to comfort or help others), while others may seem inherently evil (to covet others' spouses or possessions). But human beings are experts at white-washing our basest desires and justifying our sins. Even notably "good people" are susceptible to such biases. As Romans 3:23 reminds us, "For everyone has sinned: we all fall short of God's glorious standard."

In his book *The Righteous Mind: Why Good People Are Divided by Politics and Religion*, social psychologist Jonathan Haidt titled a subchapter, "We lie, cheat, and justify so well that we honestly believe we are honest." Haidt cites a series of experiments on cheating and concludes: "The bottom line is that in lab experiments that give people invisibility combined with plausible deniability, most people cheat. . . . Most of these cheaters leave the experiment as convinced of their own virtue as when they walked in."[2] He further argues that our "conscious reasoning functions like a press secretary who automatically justifies any position taken by the president."[3]

Evil desires are inherent to the post-fall human condition. And human beings are prone to a form of self-deceit that convinces us that many of those desires are actually good. Evil desires tend to be deeply rooted in self-interest and are often confused with or disguised as virtuous aims. Let's explore this a bit.

Take the seemingly virtuous desire of providing comfort or help to others with a hug or thoughtful touch. There's certainly nothing wrong with that. But sometimes what starts as a touch or hug (driven by a desire to provide comfort) eventually leads to sexual exploitation (which is driven by a desire for one's own sexual gratification). We all know stories of pastors, counselors, teachers, and others in "helping professions" who have abused their positions as helpers in this way.

Or consider the desire for justice. What could be more virtuous than that? But what you might try to pass off as a desire for "justice" may be little more than a manifestation of your own envy ("It's unfair for you to have more or better things than I do"), your craving for vengeance ("Because of the pain you inflicted on me, I should be able to inflict pain on you"), or your self-righteousness ("Look how good I am because of all I'm doing to pursue justice").

Some of our virtuous desires become counterproductive as they grow in strength or intensity. Too much of a good thing can become a bad thing. A desire to achieve, for example, can be a tremendous asset to a person, driving them through and beyond obstacles that would block the progress of others. So, if you are a church leader, you might have a strong drive or desire to reach lost souls for Christ. Of course, that's a good thing. But perhaps you've heard stories, as we have, of such singularly focused church leaders, pursuing that same virtuous aim, yet doing so in a way that leaves a wake of emotional and relational devastation throughout their organizations. What may have started as a desire to *achieve* gradually builds into a desire to achieve *at all costs*, which ultimately proves destructive.

● ● ●

There are times when we experience multiple desires operating simultaneously. Depending on how aligned those desires are with respect to the potentially risky behavior under consideration, they can together fuel *resolve* to act, *reluctance* to act, or *prolonged indecision*.

Every fisherman knows that the only thing worse than not catching fish is not catching fish when everyone else around you *is* catching fish. I (Rob) particularly enjoy catching bluefish from the piers in Nags Head, North Carolina. On a good day, large schools of bluefish will periodically pass under the pier in "feeding frenzies." During a feeding frenzy, the fish are so aggressive that nearly anything you throw into the water will prompt an attack. But the frenzies come and go very quickly. If you're fast and skilled enough, you might extract several fish from one school, but if you miss your chance when the school comes through, you're out of luck.

One of the best lures for catching bluefish is a Got-Cha Plug. These lures have two sets of barbed treble hooks. Bluefish also have razor sharp teeth and will try to bite you, so you must be cautious when removing the hook. During a feeding frenzy, just about every fisherman on the pier stands shoulder to shoulder casting Got-Cha Plugs into the passing schools. It is a frantic scene of rapid casting, tangled lines, toothy fish, jubilation, and swearing. It's an incredible thrill, but a lot can go wrong.

I show up at the pier with two essential desires: catch fish and avoid injury. These desires tend to compete with one another when the bluefish are running. If you want to catch fish, you must press into the mayhem of flying lures and frantic fishermen. I always wear sunglasses to protect my eyes from flying lures and carry pliers so I can remove hooks without getting bitten. I'm pretty squirrelly about human injuries. Though I am perfectly comfortable harvesting and field-dressing a deer, I usually get queasy at the mere sight of human blood or broken bones, and even passed out once while having blood drawn.

One morning when a bluefish frenzy was under way, I managed to get a nice fish on my first cast. Both sets of treble hooks had penetrated into the fish past the barbs, so it was difficult to remove the lure. I couldn't spare the time required to remove the lure carefully. In my haste, I pulled forcefully to separate the lure from the fish. The lure came out of the fish, but now it was lodged in my shorts. I was wasting precious time. The fish were biting, and I needed to get my line in the water.

With my pliers, I pulled forcefully on the lure to disentangle it from my shorts. It came free on the third tug, but the tension on the line caused it to snap back and it was now lodged in my finger tip, with the hook buried in my flesh slightly past the barb. I looked up and saw that the fish were still feeding, but couldn't very well cast my lure into the water as long as it was stuck in my finger. As my desire to catch fish overrode my desire to avoid injury, I ripped the hook from my finger and got back to fishing. I managed to catch another fish before the frenzy had passed.

As things were winding down, the guy next to me said, "Dude, you know you're bleeding all over the pier." My finger took a while to heal, but I didn't care much—I caught fish! Foolish risk? I don't think so. Sometimes multiple desires are at work simultaneously in any given situation. You've got to decide which desire to suppress and which to pursue.

● ● ●

If you want to make good decisions, the starting point is to confront the first proposition of risk in a manner that seeks the interests of God and other people over the interests of self. It seems rather simple, yet human proneness to sin and our uncanny inclination toward self-deception often prevent us from answering this question appropriately. Fundamentally, the sinful condition of the human heart is about disordered desires. We do not naturally desire the right things, and thus, we do not naturally approach this proposition in a godly way. Our desires must be shaped by God's Word and God's Spirit, over the course of time, so that we can answer this question in a godly way.

Tragically, sin and self-deception have brought about the tragic downfall of some of our most notable leaders. Many of us can name multiple Christian leaders we have admired and been helped by who have, in the past few years, been removed from their positions of leadership and destroyed their reputations because of credible allegations of serious sin and abuses of power.

Conversely, we can only wonder how many potential leaders have forfeited a life of extraordinary impact because their fear (essentially their desire to avoid failure, loss, or embarrassment) steered them away from healthy risks. Like the lazy servant described in Matthew 25, they've buried the treasures God trusted to their care *in fear of what they might lose*. It's difficult to name names here because we just don't know the things that could have happened, but didn't. There's no story of impact to tell and therefore no would-be protagonist to speak of.

• • •

We know of no *foolproof* procedures or formulas to *guarantee* you will make the right use of your desires as you evaluate any given risk-based decision. But here are a few principles and practices that can help you deal with the first proposition, *"What would you like?"* in a healthy fashion.

First, you must **acknowledge your vulnerability**. On one hand, there may be times when you simply allow your fears or lack of confidence in God's sovereignty and love to hold you back from risks that you really ought to consider taking. Yet on the other, no matter what you have achieved for the kingdom of God or how many others you have encouraged, led, or otherwise drawn nearer to God—whether you are the smartest person in the room, the most gifted communicator, the richest, whether you're a recognized expert in some area, the most well-connected, or the person everyone else goes to for advice—*you are really not that special and are certainly no less immune to sinful desires and behavior than anyone else.*

In light of that, you can next **present your desires to God**. Lay them out before him. Subject them to honest prayer. The psalmist models this for us: "Search me, O God, and know my heart; test me and know my anxious thoughts. Point out anything in me that offends you, and lead me along the path of everlasting life" (Ps. 139:23–24).

Paul encourages us similarly in Philippians 4:6–8 and challenges us to focus our thoughts and desires on goodness.

> Don't worry about anything; instead, pray about everything. Tell God what you need, and thank him for all he has done. Then you will experience God's peace, which exceeds

> anything we can understand. His peace will guard your hearts and minds as you live in Christ Jesus. And now, dear brothers and sisters, one final thing. Fix your thoughts on what is true, and honorable, and right, and pure, and lovely, and admirable. Think about things that are excellent and worthy of praise.

True, honorable, right, pure, lovely, admirable, excellent, praiseworthy. Treat each of those words as a standard by which to evaluate your desires pertaining to any risk-based decision. That's quite a gauntlet to run.

Third, we suggest you momentarily **adopt the voice of a cynic**. What we mean by this is to take a good look in the mirror and argue *against* the virtue of each of your desires and each of the risks under consideration. A cynic believes that only selfishness drives human actions. We're not cynics, but we see value in taking the *position of a cynic*, from time to time, as a tool for making wise decisions. In hearing your desires, designs, and justifications, the cynic poses hard questions and accuses your potential fears and self-interests.

> *You're just afraid.*
>
> *You just want more money for yourself.*
>
> *You're just trying to seduce her.*
>
> *You just want to feel important.*

You just have to be in charge.

(You get the picture.)

We know this sounds harsh, and we don't recommend this approach if you are prone to self-loathing or depression. But if you can honestly withstand the voice of the cynic, you'll minimize the likelihood of acting in self-interest.

Finally, **enlist the aid of others**. Proverbs 15:22 states, "Plans fail for lack of counsel, but with many advisors they succeed" (NIV). If you are reluctant or feel you cannot let anyone else into what you are thinking, that in itself is a red flag that you may be on the wrong track. Invite that person (or those persons) to grill you against the standard set forth in Philippians 4, or to play the cynic,

> We're not cynics, but we see value in taking the *position of a cynic*, from time to time, as a tool for making wise decisions.

with respect to your thoughts and desires. Whenever you are tempted to deal with a risk-based decision privately or secretly, that may be a warning sign that you are about to act foolishly.

Every risk ever taken had its root in desire. But are the circumstances, conditions, or situation suitable for that desire to be realized? We'll turn to that question in the next proposition.

CHAPTER 6

PROPOSITION 2: "WHAT IS AVAILABLE?"

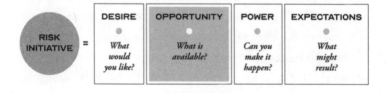

It makes little sense to speak of *taking a risk* absent any desire to exchange what *is* for what *might be*. We *risk* in the interest and hope of changing or improving something. And that implies a desire.

So you have this desire (for food, money, comfort, sex, power, growth). Now the second proposition comes into play: *Okay, what might be available to satisfy that desire?*

In making decisions and taking risks, the second proposition concerns *opportunity*. Opportunity is about the *circumstances* (conditions or situational factors) that create the potential to advance any given desire, and the array of *options* available for doing so. This proposition may be experienced as either a question ("What is available?") or an invitation ("Here's what's available").

That we've placed this proposition second rather than first is not to say that you'd never experience "What is available?" before "What would you like?" Sometimes risk-based decisions are proposed to us in just that sequence, in which case the opportunity (second proposition) may serve to *awaken* our desire (first proposition). That billboard that you passed on the way to work, announcing the current lottery jackpot amount, is an example of this. You may have been driving along without presently giving any thought to getting rich, but the billboard confronts and awakens that desire for wealth. Most advertising works that way—it puts forth proposition 2 ("Here's what's available") under the assumption that a good percentage of those reached by the ad have an underlying desire (proposition 1) for food, money, comfort, sex, fame, power, respect—which the advertised product or service can fulfill.

We've simply chosen to place the opportunity proposition after the desire proposition because the mere existence of opportunity implies an objective (a goal or object of your desire) and raises the question, "opportunity for what?" An opportunity is only truly an opportunity insofar as it might serve to fulfill an existing desire.

• • •

Proposition 2—*opportunity*—is about circumstances or options. Circumstances encompass conditions and situational factors in which we find or place ourselves. It's that recognition of "Well, here we are . . . here's what's available . . . here's what we have to work with."

In the book of Acts, we read about an encounter between the apostle Philip and an Ethiopian eunuch he meets along the road that connects Jerusalem to Gaza. Philip finds the man reading an ancient prophecy from the book of Isaiah and asks him if he understands what he is reading. The eunuch replies, "How can I unless someone explains it to me?" (Acts 8:31 NIV). Philip goes on to illuminate the passage and tells the eunuch the good news about Jesus. The eunuch embraces the good news and chooses to follow Jesus, as the story picks up:

> As they rode along, they came to some water, and the eunuch said, "Look! There's some water! Why can't I be baptized?" He ordered the carriage to stop, and they went down into the water, and Philip baptized him. (8:36–38)

The newly converted eunuch had a *desire* to follow Jesus. He recognized baptism as an important act of discipleship. When he found himself by some water—*Here's what's available, a body of water*—he wasted no time in making use of the circumstances to fulfill his desire. We have no indication that the eunuch pulled out an ancient map to search for a nearby body of water. He appears to have simply happened upon it as he was traveling.

Like the Ethiopian eunuch, we sometimes unintentionally find ourselves in situations where there is exposure to risk. Or, as the esteemed theologian, Curly Howard, might put it, *"I'm a victim of soycomstance!"* Here are some examples of the kinds of circumstances that might come upon us:

- There I was pushing my cart through the grocery store when I looked up and saw the man who sexually abused me as a child.
- I looked down and found a $20 bill on the sidewalk.
- I came upon the scene of a car accident.
- I came down with a dangerous virus.
- I heard someone calling for help.
- I received a call from a church member who wants to donate a new organ to our music ministry.
- A little-known business leader has been nominated to serve on our church board.
- A teacher stopped me in the atrium between gatherings and asked about employment opportunities to work with kids at the church.

- A struggling downtown church called and wants to give us their building.
- A fairly new and opinionated church attendee would like to make a large donation to the church.

• • •

Now let's look at another side of opportunity. Let's go beyond the circumstances or situational factors pertinent to risk-based decisions and consider the options or choices that might be available in any given set of circumstances. Let's look at the component of proposition 2—*What is available?*—that pertains to the array of *options or choices* available to satisfy a desire.

Suppose you were hungry and decided to go to a restaurant in order to fulfill your desire to eat. Of course, if you're at the restaurant, you've already dealt with the second proposition on some level, as you have rejected other options for dealing with your desire to eat, like cooking a meal at home, having leftovers, foraging through the woods behind your house for mushrooms and berries, or fasting.

But for simplicity's sake, let's just pick up on your risk-based decision from the point where you receive the menu. Receiving the menu is the second proposition to risk in the *option* form. It is a list of "what is available" to eat. Most of us order food so routinely that we don't view our selections as risk-based decision-making. Granted, the level of risk in such situations—the degree of exposure to the chance of injury or loss—is generally pretty low. But every once in a while, people end up suffering through a meal that tastes pretty bad, or they start feeling unwell an hour or two later, and sometimes they experience a dangerous reaction like food poisoning or a severe food allergy. So, ordering food from a menu is a risk-based decision, despite the level of risk being fairly low.

We find it useful to think in terms of three different kinds of options or choices:

1. Duh Options. Choices or opportunities of this type are readily apparent to the average person. They appear on the list of "what is available" almost as plainly as any item printed on a restaurant menu. "If you wish to eat here, these are your choices." You don't have to be particularly creative or perceptive to see these opportunities. They are the obvious options.

So, let's say you just received an inheritance of $20,000. Some of the duh opportunities might include: putting the money in a savings account, paying off existing debt, investing in the stock market, buying something for yourself, donating to charity, or apportioning $4,000 to each of those five things.

Or let's consider a situation where you have a low-paying job and desire to earn more income. Your duh opportunities might include these options: asking for a raise, asking for a promotion, applying for a job someplace else, picking up a side gig, or getting additional education or training so that you'll qualify for a higher-paying job. Each of these opportunities may come with its own set of potential consequences that must be carefully weighed, but the opportunities themselves are readily apparent.

2. Devised Options. Choices or opportunities of this type are created, discovered, or invented. They appear on the list of "what is available" not because they are obvious or set in front of the decision maker by some external source (as in the case of the Ethiopian eunuch), but because the decision maker was able to *generate* them. In our menu analogy, these are the special-order items. You have to veer off the menu to get them. "I see the brisket platter comes with fresh-cut fries. Can I substitute sweet potato fries instead?" "My five-year-old daughter won't eat anything on the menu. Could you please see if the cook is willing to make a grilled cheese sandwich for her?"

We find that many breakaway leaders and successful entrepreneurs have a knack for seeing and creating options that others do not. They don't necessarily make high-maintenance customers in a restaurant, but when faced with leadership challenges or business opportunities, they tend not to settle for the usual array of menu items. These individuals seem particularly good at actively generating conditions that set the stage or create potential for them to act upon their desires.

> Many breakaway leaders and successful entrepreneurs have a knack for seeing and creating options that others do not.

When we find ourselves in situations or circumstances that we have actively created, we cannot honestly claim that the given situation *came upon us*—we have essentially devised additional options or pathways toward risky behavior. Here are some examples of the kinds of circumstances we might actively generate:

- I'm going to do a Google search for that guy I dated in high school.
- If I volunteer to clean up trash at the park this weekend, I may get a chance to share my faith with someone.
- Let's go to that club where celebrities hang out.
- I've booked a big game hunt in Zambia.
- I'm going to look for a new job.

As we speak of devised options, it is important to recognize that creating circumstances favorable to risk is not the same thing as actually taking risk. Googling a high school sweetheart does not make marital infidelity a foregone conclusion, nor does sending that person a friend request. But both actions alter circumstances in a way that increase the risk of infidelity—and they reflect poorly on the first proposition, your desires. Perhaps you haven't stopped to ask yourself, *Why am I making this decision?* Volunteering at a park does not constitute sharing your faith, but it is likely to create conditions that will enable you to share your faith. So, devised options are willfully produced circumstances, driven by one's desires, that increase the likelihood of risky behavior.

Located in a small, rural farming community, local township leaders felt that LCBC Church, now having grown to more than 6,000 weekly attendees, had become a strain on its road system. Additionally, in its never-ending battle to preserve its farmland, the decision was made not to grant permission for the church to add to its existing property or buildings. Once again, church leaders were faced with the question, "Are we done introducing more people to Jesus, or does God have more in store for us?"

About that same time, we (David and staff) began hearing about a handful of churches around the country who, rather than building bigger buildings, were finding success opening new locations through the use of video teaching. After a quick cross-country trip to visit several of these brand-new "multi-site" churches and to see what opportunities might be available to us, we decided to take the risk and jump into the multi-site world.

But it almost never got off the ground. Having identified our top five communities that seemed prime for a new LCBC campus, we set out to find the same amount of property that would allow us to build the same size building and accommodate the same number of people as our original campus. For two years we searched in vain. Our plans stalled.

Then, while meeting with a cohort of other hopeful multi-site churches, we were challenged to reconsider our expectations, and work with what was available in these five communities. They said, "Rather than start with a facility that would come at a great expense to accommodate 6,000 people (6,000 people we didn't yet have), why not start by renting a small venue and see what happens?"

So, we found a school to rent on the weekends, and we slipped (not jumped) into the world of multi-site churches. Three hundred people showed up our first weekend. A year later a venue became available in a community we had not targeted, and 700 people came out to open our third location. Now, with nineteen locations spread across Eastern Pennsylvania, we have twice as many people engaging with LCBC *away* from our original campus as at our original campus.

More recently, what's available changed, and that change brought with it more opportunity. Like most other churches across the country, LCBC shut its doors due to COVID restrictions. Our world changed. We worried whether or not we could withstand such a lockdown. We braced ourselves for catastrophic financial losses. And we were forced to work with the only thing available at the time—the internet and online church.

We worked with what we had to work with, and now, though our buildings are refilling, we have as many people attending LCBC Church online as in our buildings. This was definitely an off-menu order.

A word of caution is in order here. That same tendency seen among breakaway leaders and entrepreneurs to devise opportunities that are not obvious to others has a dark side. When tainted by self-interest, it can lead them to pursue opportunities to risk in areas that satisfy some of their *less-than-honorable desires*. That same talent for out-of-the-box thinking may be used to manufacture opportunities that only serve to enrich themselves, gratify their sexual desires outside of their own marriages, eliminate rivals, fuel their pride or stature, and so on.

3. Deleted Options. Much as we can *devise* options, we can also choose to *delete* or limit them. Opportunities of this type are preemptively omitted or avoided. They are deliberately *removed* from the menu. In our restaurant menu analogy, this is where you have decided for one reason or another that some items on the menu are categorically off-limits. Maybe you are lactose or gluten intolerant, are trying to lose weight, or have an allergy to certain foods. Maybe you're just philosophically opposed (as is Rob) to any food that contains kale, chickpeas, or tofu. What might be a reasonable and obvious option or opportunity for others is intentionally deleted or disqualified.

Former vice president Mike Pence famously stated that he will not place himself in circumstances where he is alone with another woman, nor will he attend an event where alcohol is being served unless his wife is present. He states he adopted this practice in the interest of keeping his marriage strong and healthy. We imagine that if we were to press him on the matter, his rationale might be something like, "If I don't allow myself to be alone with a woman or be in situations where there are lots of people who have reduced their inhibitions by drinking alcohol, then I'm not likely to behave in a sexually inappropriate way nor otherwise fall into any temptation of marital infidelity." In other words, he goes to greater lengths than most others in eliminating certain opportunities to cheat on his wife.

Mr. Pence seems to recognize that his desire for sexual intimacy (which is a healthy, God-given desire made for the marital relationship) could lead to damaging risky behavior, and so he has preemptively limited his opportunities to satisfy the dark aspects of that desire. His critics argue that this practice of Mr. Pence's effectively discriminates against women by restricting their access to his power and influence. While there might be some merit to that argument, certainly there are other avenues he could create in order to provide effective access for women that would easily offset that bias (for instance, create group meetings and group mentoring opportunities where the ratio of women participants is higher than that of men).

• • •

Whether you are a high-ranking politician, an ordinary person on the street, or somewhere in between, you'll want to confront the second proposition of risk, *What is available?* (opportunity), in a way that is wise and pleasing to God. Ask God to help you see circumstances and choices that advance his purposes, to eliminate counterproductive fears, and to protect you from circumstances that will leave you vulnerable to foolish and destructive risks.

If you have come through the first proposition with confidence that your desires are constructive and healthy, yet are still struggling to find a path toward fulfilling those desires, then:

- Consider waiting for better timing. Circumstances may change.
- Avoid getting locked into a limited number of options. There are usually more than readily meet the eye.
- Ask yourself, *Is there some option(s) I may be overlooking? Can I make or generate something new . . . that I didn't think could exist?*

Breakaway leaders and other entrepreneurs tend to be particularly good at this. Talk with someone in a different field with a wildly different way of thinking from yours. Press yourself to identify other possibilities. Doing so may help you see your opportunity with a new set of eyes.

You may also consider, *Would it be wise to preemptively prevent or constrain myself from making choices in my personal vulnerability areas, so that in the heat of the moment I don't do something foolish?* Are their circumstances you should actively avoid or options you should preemptively eliminate?

If you have played or watched baseball, you're familiar with the concept of a warning track. The warning track on a baseball field is a strip or band of gravel or similar surface, several feet wide, that separates the grassy playing field from the fence. It forms a boundary around the playing field and serves as a buffer zone between the field and the fence or wall. When fielders are chasing pop-ups or fly balls, they must keep an eye on the ball if they expect to make the catch. Take your eye off the ball, and you're not going to catch it. The warning track signals fielders, who may be running full-speed in pursuit of the ball, that they are getting close to the wall and better slow down if they don't want to crash and hurt themselves.

Consider how you might use this warning track concept, figuratively, to guard against potentially destructive risk-taking. Should you, like Mike Pence, avoid being alone with persons of the opposite sex? Should you put a windowpane in your office door? Should you invite another person to monitor what you spend money on? Should you give your spouse location monitoring access to your cell phone? Should you be "blind" as to who donates what amounts to your ministry? One person's warning track is not the same as the next. It's primarily up to you as a leader to take an honest look at your vulnerabilities and to set those boundaries.

As with the first proposition ("*What would you like?*"), dealing with the second proposition ("*What is available?*") in a constructive manner, requires that you be alert to your vulnerabilities and your strengths. We've said it before: whether you are the smartest person in the room, the most gifted communicator, the richest, or if you're a recognized expert in some area, the most well-connected or the person everyone else goes to for advice—*you are no less immune to sinful desires and behavior than anyone else.*

But there's a flip side. Even if you're not particularly brilliant, credentialed, connected, or resourced, God has nonetheless given you valuable treasure to invest (to place at risk, to do something with) on his behalf. That brings us to the next proposition: *"Can you make it happen?"*

CHAPTER 7

PROPOSITION 3: "CAN YOU MAKE IT HAPPEN?"

When you think of powerful people, you probably envision politicians, corporate executives, celebrities, military leaders, judges, crime bosses, and people of great wealth—the movers and shakers of the world who convince, control, and exert dominion over the rest of us. By comparison, you may not feel very powerful at all.

Okay, so maybe your decisions don't show up on the daily news, and hardly anyone follows you on social media. But chances are, you have a lot more power than you realize.

The third proposition in making good decisions and taking wise risks concerns *power*. In any decision where risk is involved—where failure might reasonably result in some form of injury or loss—we face the question, "Can you make it happen? Can you pull it off? Do you have the capacity, the clout, and the ability to attain what you desire?"

Power comes down to your capacity to make a difference . . . to affect the world around you. Your power derives from many different sources. Your physical size and strength give you a certain degree of power over anyone who is smaller or weaker than yourself. So, if you are an average-sized healthy adult, you possess physical power over virtually any young child or elderly adult. You can make that child or elderly person do certain things, or constrain them from doing certain things, simply because you are more physically powerful than they are.

You can use that power responsibly—for example, to scoop up your three-year-old son who, in the midst of a tantrum, is hurling building blocks at another toddler, or to assist your frail octogenarian grandparent in climbing stairs or entering a car safely. Or you can use that power irresponsibly, in a manner that is physically harsh or abusive.

Your position or status in your company or within some other social structure can be a source of power. Likewise, your intellect, persuasive abilities, wealth, fame, specialized skills, reputation, and connections with influential people all play into the power you possess—your capacity to pull things off, make a difference, affect the world around you. These attributes may heavily influence your answer to proposition 3: *"Can you make it happen?"*

For the most part, you can expect your power to increase as you advance your career and accrue life achievements. As you build reputation and relationships. As you become seasoned and successful.

Consider a typical pastor. Most of the pastors we know are not wealthy. They may have relatively few paid employees under their leadership, so they don't feel like the boss of anything substantial. But even pastors of small churches have at least several dozen people looking to them for moral guidance and spiritual leadership and willing to spend at least an hour or so each week to hear their perspective on all sorts of practical matters.

Part-time youth pastors have students looking up to them—students who crave whatever time and attention they have to give. Parents look to them for advice on how to deal with some situation involving their teen at home. When pastors use their power in healthy ways, good things happen. People in their congregations grow spiritually and infect their communities (and maybe even communities in faraway places) with love and good deeds. That's power, isn't it?

Healthy leaders embrace the power they have to make a difference. They can see value in accruing even more power, insofar as they do so through honorable means. They recognize that we serve a God of possibilities who consistently acts out of love for his people. When confronted with risk-based decisions, they know they both are dependent upon and can draw upon God's power. So, they are prone to reframe the third proposition, *Can you make it happen?*, into something like, *Can God use me to make it happen?* They might respond with something like, "God can make that happen, and I believe he can use me to do it."

Faith can cure uncertainty or unhealthy risk aversion. Yet it should not lead us to underestimate negative consequences. Good people still run into hardship and experience failure. God never promised that our lives would be all sunshine and roses. He never promised that everything born out of good intention would turn to gold. Faith is knowing that God is in control, that he knows what he's doing, and that he consistently acts in love toward his people. That assurance can reduce our irrational fears and help keep our risks in proper perspective.

> Faith is knowing that God is in control, that he knows what he's doing, and that he consistently acts in love toward his people.

For those of us prone to self-doubt, part of the issue may be that we're simply too self-focused—exaggerating our own influence in the grand scheme of God's sovereign plans and too concerned that the *outcomes* we experience in any particular decision or situation will define us as a success or a failure in life. God is more concerned with our character (which falls on us) than the outcome of our efforts (which falls on him).

Good leaders realize they must sometimes wield their power in ways that cause hurt or pain to others. They judiciously opt to inflict what amounts to harm or injury to themselves or some other person or constituency in the interest of advancing a greater cause or purpose.

So, as a leader, you might have to cancel a vacation on short notice because of a crisis in your organization that requires you to be present and visible. You might have to fire some really nice people who simply cannot perform their jobs adequately. You may have to shut down a program or service line that was accomplishing some positive things in order to make room in your budget for something else that you believe will more effectively advance your organization's mission.

You won't do any of those things to be mean or to inflict pain. You'll do them to keep your church or company functioning well. You'll weigh the risks and sometimes make hard, painful, but necessary choices. Leaders who cannot stomach those kinds of risks are not likely to shepherd their organizations toward extraordinary performance. Individuals who cannot stomach these risks are not likely to achieve high levels of growth in their personal lives.

• • •

During the summer between my junior and senior years of college, I (Rob) had an internship at a facility that provided outpatient day treatment services to adults with serious and persistent mental health disorders—people with chronic schizophrenia, severe bipolar disorders, and the like.

One Friday afternoon, I took off early to visit a friend for the weekend. I didn't own a car at the time, so I decided to take the bus. I arrived early at the station, as I did not want to risk missing my bus. While waiting there, one of the patients from the facility, whom I'll call Alan, wandered in and bought a ticket. I knew him fairly well and had some concern for what he might be up to, as Alan was actively symptomatic (e.g., experiencing auditory hallucinations, disorganized speech, inappropriate emotional responses, social skill deficits, poor judgment).

So, I struck up a conversation, casually asking him where he was headed and what he had planned for the weekend. Alan had some obvious motor tics and tended to speak loudly and behave in a manner that drew attention to himself. I quickly surmised (as did everyone else in the bus station) that Alan was headed to New York City where he had relatives, but he had no idea where they actually lived nor how to contact them. He did not tell his family he was leaving. He had $200 "right here in my pocket." He did not have his medication. He did not know his way around New York.

I thought to myself, *Holy cow, this guy is going to get hurt if he goes to New York City. I've got to protect him. I've got to stop him.* I had a risk-based decision to make:

> *What would you like?*—I want Alan to be safe. (Proposition #1—Desire)
>
> *What is available?*—I've got Alan wrapped up in a conversation at the bus station. I can let him go or try to keep him from going. (Proposition #2—Opportunity)
>
> *Can you make it happen?*—Yes, I have the power to stop him. He's pretty easy to distract. (Proposition #3—Power)

So I kept Alan talking. I asked one question after another on whatever topic came to my mind. The bus to New York had arrived at the terminal. I kept Alan talking. The bus to New York was now boarding. I kept Alan talking. The bus to New York would now be departing. I kept Alan talking.

When I was sure the bus was far enough that it would not come back to get him, I said something to the effect of: "Wait, you were heading to New York, right? Ah man, I think that bus already left." Alan checked at the window and returned very upset with himself for missing the bus. He said he would be heading back home. When he left, I called into the office and spoke with his caseworker so that she would be aware of the situation.

I thought I had done my good deed. I cared about Alan and wanted him to stay safe, so I tricked him into missing his bus. When I got back after the weekend, I learned that Alan's case worker had contacted Alan's family to report the incident. They knew nothing of Alan's plans and were appreciative that I had stopped him from leaving town.

I later heard that Alan received a severe beating from his brother for what he had done.

The risk I took in preventing Alan from traveling to the big city, with the intention of keeping him safe from harm, had totally backfired. My actions actually caused harm rather than preventing it. In retrospect, I am saddened by the *result*, but I don't regret the *decision*.

Even good decisions sometimes yield unfortunate results. Every "good risk" brings the *possibility* of a bad outcome. Leaders must expect and accept occasional failure.

● ● ●

As your power increases, it may happen in subtle ways that you might not recognize. As a pastor or ministry leader, you are seen by people as an expert on the Bible and on life more generally, and they may hang onto your words more than you realize.

And since ministry work is resourced by donated money and time, you probably devote considerable time to recruiting volunteers and conducting fundraising of some kind or another. That tends to place you around "important people"—people who are talented and well-resourced. Your influence on them can be compounded as it impacts how they behave, spend their time, run their organizations, and donate their money. Some of those people may invite you to use their vacation homes, play golf at their country clubs, or invite you to social gatherings where you'll meet other influential people.

At first you'll feel like a fish out of water, but then it will feel normal, and before long, you might get to thinking *you're* pretty important.

If your ministry grows and you don't do foolish things to derail your career, then your influence—your power—will expand in even greater ways. That's a really good thing to the extent that you use that power to serve God and others.

As your power increases, you will be more prone to answering "yes" to the third proposition—*"Can you make it happen?"*

- Yes, I can lead that project.
- Yes, I can make that presentation.
- Yes, I can get a meeting with the mayor.
- Yes, I can handle that job.
- Yes, I can persuade that donor.
- Yes, I can protect that child.
- Yes, I can build this organization.
- Yes, I can manipulate that co-worker for sexual pleasure.
- Yes, I can buy things for myself on the company card.

- Yes, I can force my subordinate to do things my way.
- Yes, I can keep that person from talking.
- Yes, I can enrich myself by steering that contract.

As you gain power, you must become increasingly vigilant about your own propensity to become an abuser of power. In other words, as your power grows, you are more likely to abuse it. This happens for all kinds of people in powerful positions—the ones who write the books, give the keynotes at leadership conferences. Indeed, the very persons we seek to emulate.

Why is it that so many well-reputed and seemingly good people, at the height of their influence, begin to abuse their power? What happens to these exemplars of effective leadership that causes them to become bullies, embezzlers, and sexual predators? Why do so many standard-bearers turn out to be scoundrels? What causes strong leaders to act as though they had ingested what one friend described as "crazy pills"? And how do you prevent yourself from joining their ranks?

It turns out there is a lot of truth in the adage that power corrupts. In his book *The Power Paradox,* psychology professor Dacher Keltner argues that groups give power to certain individuals because they are nice people who look out for others' needs and advance the greater good. But Keltner also argues that power is seductive, and that as people gain power, they reliably tend to lose their sense of empathy and begin to abuse their power.

Keltner's team's research demonstrates that power corrupts in four ways. It leads to: (1) empathy deficits and diminished moral sentiments; (2) self-serving impulsivity; (3) incivility and disrespect; and (4) a sense of personal exceptionalism (the notion that the rules should apply to everyone except themselves).[4]

As we gain power, we become more self-centered and less capable of appreciating the feelings and viewpoints of others; we're more prone to act on our desires and impulses, to speak our minds and make risky choices and gambles; we're more likely to interrupt, tease, critique, and humiliate others; and more likely to see ourselves as exceptional and special.

You don't have to look hard to find people in power who overestimate their own virtue, who engage in instrumental aggression (hostile-looking behavior in order to achieve what they see as a worthwhile goal), or who take credit for their team's accomplishments. In short, it's the nice people who are granted power by others, but as their power increases, their niceness decreases, and they tend to abuse the power they've been given.

Pastors and other good people like to believe they're immune to those influences, but they're not. We're all vulnerable to seeing ourselves as increasingly important over time, as our accomplishments begin to stack up and our power increases.

Don't be surprised that as your church or ministry attains a higher profile, you occasionally fall into thinking it's because of *your* leadership, because of what *you've* done. People will tell you you're a good teacher, a good leader, a good man or woman. At some point perhaps, other leaders will invite you to teach them to do at their churches what you do at yours. People will talk you up and treat you special, and you'll sometimes start believing your own hype.

Realistically, if you are in a significant leadership position, you probably are better at a lot of things than most people around you. As a pastor, you might get to thinking you are more articulate, persuasive, entertaining, and perhaps even smarter or wiser than the average person in your congregation. There's a grain of truth to that, or you wouldn't be succeeding in your work.

But the danger is when we move from acknowledging that God has gifted us to be *better at certain things* than many others, to thinking we're actually *better than others*. Or we might forget that our talents are truly *gifts*. As Paul asked the Corinthian believers, "What do you have that God hasn't given you? And if everything you have is from God, why boast as though it were not a gift?" (1 Cor. 4:7). In other words, *the only reason you're good at anything is because God made you good at it, and he can take away that gift if he wants!*

Just because our gifts put us in the limelight doesn't mean they're greater than the kinds of gifts that enable one to serve in a less noticeable fashion. It can be difficult to keep all of that in proper perspective, and you sometimes let your confidence, which is a good thing, drift into arrogance, which is not.

• • •

From my first day at LCBC Church, I (David) began studying churches (and businesses) that were a few steps ahead of us,
and I continue that practice today. Four months into my new role
as pastor at LCBC, I rounded up our Board of Elders and took
them on a two-hour drive into Philadelphia where we attended
together a "Breaking the 200 Barrier" conference.

Once we had broken the 200-member barrier, we began
observing churches of 400–600 people, preparing ourselves for
what it might take to lead a church of 400. But we also needed
a bigger dream of what could be, of what God could do if we
continued to follow his leading. So I began to take our leaders to
observe and visit churches of 10,000 and 12,000 people.

We came away from those visits with mixed feelings. First,
we came away depressed. "We'll never have that many people—
such nice facilities—that many volunteers—that much money—
that good of a sound system—that strong of a staff!"

We also came away inspired. "Surely if God could do that
there—with those people—in that location—with those leaders—he could do it here as well!"

But we also came home in awe. In awe of what God had
done, but also in awe of the leaders of those massive churches.
"Surely they must be smarter than us—more gifted than us—
more energetic than us—more blessed than us!" And sometimes
we even wondered, "What's wrong with us?!?"

That sense of awe and wonder continued until LCBC began to grow into a similar size church, at times even surpassing some of the churches we had both secretly cherished and despised! And as we began to have the opportunity to connect personally more and more with the leaders of these churches, we came to the startling realization that "Those leaders are just like us!" Yes, they are smart. Yes, they are gifted. Yes, they are driven. And yes, they may even be blessed. But not any more than the rest of us! After all these years of idolizing others, now we know they are just like us.

And while God has blessed our church, we constantly remind our staff, "Yes, you are smart, and yes, you are gifted, and yes, you'd better be driven—that's why we hired you! But don't ever think that just because we are a big church we are smarter, or more gifted, or better than any other church staff—we're not. And for some reason God has chosen to bless us, so let's not do anything stupid to mess up what God is doing here!"

• • •

We've been talking about breakaway leaders as being distinct from others—as being extraordinary even among leaders. But they're really not so special after all, are they? Are you? You're susceptible to the same kinds of joys, hardships, temptations, and sins as everyone else. And like everyone else, you are responsible to do the most with what God has trusted to your care, whether that comes in the form of resources, talent, or circumstances.

First Corinthians 4:7 is again a great reminder: "What do you have that God hasn't given you? And if everything you have is from God, why boast as though it were not a gift?"

Even so, you may catch yourself thinking that because you carry so much weight on your shoulders and make a lot of sacrifices for the good of your ministry, you deserve some special privilege or means of rewarding yourself—more pay, a bigger expense account, a flexible schedule, a longer or more luxurious vacation than the others on your staff. Or maybe some little indulgence having to do with food, relaxation, sexual gratification, or just spending money on things for yourself that you don't really need. The minute we start thinking we are exceptional or immune from these hazards, we wander into a dangerous zone.

We like this quote attributed to Abraham Lincoln: "Nearly all men can stand adversity, but if you want to test a man's character, give him power."

As your power grows, make use of it, but do so with great caution. You must guard against its potential to corrupt you. Failing to do so can undo a lifetime of good and honorable work, as we have seen time and time again.

Remember to lean on *God's* power and love, and trust in his intention to use you.

Recognize the strength that comes with that, yet also the vulnerability that comes with being a sinful creature . . . just like every other human on the face of the earth.

Foster relationships with a loving critic or two—people who will confront you, ask the tough questions, challenge your motives and your actions.

Actively invite checks on your power—from your board, your elders, your colleagues, or a small group of trusted friends. Offer accountability and transparency even if they are not asked of you.

Desire, opportunity, and power. Three distinct propositions of risk. Three key ingredients that will present themselves in any risk-based decision you might ever face. The final proposition of risk—expectations—offers your last line of defense against foolish risks and against the fears that can hold you back from taking healthy risks.

CHAPTER 8

PROPOSITION 4: "WHAT MIGHT RESULT?"

	DESIRE	OPPORTUNITY	POWER	EXPECTATIONS
RISK INITIATIVE =	*What would you like?*	*What is available?*	*Can you make it happen?*	*What might result?*

Every one of us goes about every day of our lives repeatedly predicting or anticipating consequences of our actions.

As I (Rob) wrote that last sentence, I took a swig of coffee. I didn't put much conscious energy into it, but I have learned and therefore come to expect that when I run a coffee pod through my Keurig machine, a liquid substance of a certain color, temperature, and flavor will drain into my mug. Adding some cream will slightly alter the flavor, color, and temperature of that sub-stance. The mug will contain the liquid and keep it warm for a certain period of time. And if I pick up the mug and tilt it toward my mouth with my lips properly positioned, the substance will taste and feel a particular way as it enters my body.

That sequence of actions almost always produces the same result. It turns out exactly as I expect nearly every time. When our expectations are not met in a situation as reliably predict-able as this, we call it a surprise. I have found that most coffee surprises—curdled cream, lukewarm temperature, harsh flavor, unidentified flotsam—tend to be unpleasant.

The fourth proposition in making good decisions and tak-ing wise risks—*"What might result?"*—concerns *expectations*, the anticipated effects or outcomes of our choices. Whether the deci-sion at hand is as routine as sipping coffee or as consequential as a career change, your expectations—your response to the fourth proposition—come into play. If you expect an action to produce a mostly positive or desirable outcome, then you are likely to proceed. And if you expect a mostly negative or undesirable out-come, then you are likely to halt or at least hesitate.

Your expectations are a matter of both probability and mag-nitude. So, as you contend with the proposition, "What might result?" in a risk-based decision, you naturally consider one or more possible outcomes and assign a probability and magnitude to each.

I (Rob) was blessed with a very caring mother. She loved me and my siblings and wanted nothing more than to keep us safe from all the world's hazards. But it seemed that every time I thought of something fun to do, she expected me to break my neck.

> "Mom, can I climb that tree?"
>
> "No, you'll fall and break your neck."
>
> "Can I walk to Gill's Garage and buy some candy?"
>
> "No, you'll get hit by a car crossing Joppa Road and break your neck."
>
> "Can I jump off the diving board?"
>
> "No, you'll hit your head on the board or the bottom and break your neck."

I'm sure people do, on rare occasion, break their necks while climbing trees, crossing streets, and jumping into pools. And it would be horrible to suffer a broken neck. But as a child, I could see that lots of other kids did those things without breaking their necks. Breaking my neck seemed to be a low probability outcome, so I eventually wised up (at least to my way of seeing things) and stopped asking permission. This added a new potential outcome to the fourth proposition—namely, that I might get caught in a lie and punished.

• • •

It stands to reason that people who are cautious by nature, on average, suffer fewer and less adverse consequences than people who are prone to taking risks. They don't break their necks as often as daredevils do. But cautious people do pay a price. They tend to overlook the negative consequences of *not* taking risks and thereby cheat themselves out of life's joys and accomplishments.

So how do expectations come into play when normally wise and accomplished leaders take foolish risks? How could someone so smart fail to anticipate that his sexually deviant behavior might someday catch up with him? How could someone so experienced and seasoned not see the glaring contradiction between her behavior and her life's work? "*What was she thinking?*"

> Cautious people do pay a price. They tend to overlook the negative consequences of *not* taking risks and thereby cheat themselves out of life's joys and accomplishments.

To understand this, we must look at the mindset of leaders. We believe that breakaway leaders tend to be realistic optimists. Good leaders are visionary and genuinely get excited about what the future might hold. They have a realistic appreciation for adversity and barriers, but generally believe they can get beyond them. People follow leaders out of *hope* for a better future. In other words, leaders inspire others to *expect* that they can collectively bring about a better state of affairs—that by throwing in with that leader, they will have a part in causing some meaningful positive change.

Followers of breakaway leaders have expectations that might look like this:

- If I get to play with Tom Brady, I will win a Super Bowl.
- If I fight under George Patton, I will help free Europe from Nazi oppression.
- If I march with Susan B. Anthony, I will gain the full rights of citizenship.
- If I follow Martin Luther King Jr., I will help eradicate racism.
- If I join forces with this ministry leader, I will help others follow God, make the world a better place, and spend eternity in heaven.

Even the everyday leaders in our lives inspire hopeful expectations:

- If I follow my boss, our project will succeed.
- If I follow my tour guide, I will arrive at a beautiful destination.
- If I cling to my mommy's leg, that mean dog won't bite me.

A key component of every leader's job is to inspire others to expect that they can collectively bring about a better state of affairs. Some of that inspiration may come through the leader's persuasive words, but most of it comes by building a track record of success. Every quarterback says he'll win games, but Tom Brady has the rings to prove it.

Success breeds the expectation of further success. We might call that *confidence* that our choices and actions will lead to successful outcomes. Success tends to build confidence. People who have been winning generally expect to keep winning. This can help emerging leaders become increasingly effective over time. Each success can strengthen their expectation of further success, giving them the courage to take more healthy risks.

But as with the other propositions of risk, there is a serious hazard in all of this—a dark side. A track record of success can lead to overconfidence and inflated expectations and may bring about disastrous consequences. Those who have come to expect everything they touch will turn to gold are likely to start touching things they shouldn't.

This is why that business leader who was successful in one industry recklessly expects she will experience similar success in a new industry she knows nothing about. The investor who accrued wealth through real estate assumes he will do equally well as a venture capitalist or in cryptocurrency, and then loses his shirt. And that politician, pastor, athlete, or film producer sexually victimizes vulnerable women, expecting no one will find out and he'll never get caught.

The person who sees themselves as a winner starts believing they cannot possibly lose, that they can pretty much pull off anything they put their mind to. They start neglecting or overlooking their vulnerabilities and flaws—and that leads to damaging risk-taking behavior. The initial forays into unhealthy risk may be mild—perhaps a flirtatious comment, a lingering but not overtly sexual touch, overstating mileage on a travel expense log, paying cash for a drinking or gambling expense so one's spouse would not know of it.

Whenever you risk small and "get away with it" (meaning you do not experience negative consequences), your expectations are likely to change, leading you to underestimate the magnitude and/or probability of experiencing negative consequences the next time you take that kind of risk. And you may escalate the unhealthy risk-taking over time, so that the flirting and touching become overtly suggestive or sexual, the expense logs include falsified charges, and the drinking or gambling episodes become costly binges.

• • •

In his book *Good to Great* Jim Collins lays out a hierarchy of leadership capabilities, with "Level 5" referring to the highest level—those leaders who build enduring greatness. Such leaders, he says:

> . . . look out the window to apportion credit to
> factors outside themselves when things go well
> (and if they cannot find a specific person or
> event to give credit to, they credit good luck).
> At the same time, they look in the mirror to
> apportion responsibility, never blaming bad
> luck when things go poorly.[5]

Level 5 leaders—those who ultimately build enduring success—blend extreme personal humility with intense professional will. We believe it is critical that leaders maintain a humble outlook on their own success. When leaders see themselves as the sole or even primary agent of their success—neglecting the agency of God and other people—their vulnerability to foolish risks increases.

As we have said throughout, risk initiative is determined by a combination of desire, opportunity, power, and expectations—DOPE. We contend that opportunity and power tend to expand as leaders advance their careers and that a track record of success can lead to unrealistically high expectations that a leader's actions will produce positive results.

So, compared to others, leaders are better positioned to get what they want and more prone to assume or expect that the actions they take will lead to favorable outcomes. This makes it all the more important that leaders recognize their vulnerability to unhealthy desires (which we all, as sinful creatures, are subject to) and take steps to guard against their influence.

The fourth proposition, expectation, is the last line of defense against foolish risk-taking. It can also provide a final boost of encouragement to embrace healthy risk. So in confronting this proposition, it is helpful to consider the potential consequences, good and bad, of both initiating risk and avoiding it. Think in terms of both probability and magnitude. Ask yourself:

- What's the *worst* that can happen? For me personally? For other people who might be impacted by my decision?
- What are the *real odds* of that outcome?
- What's the *best* that can happen? For me personally? For other people who might be impacted by my decision?
- What are the odds of *that* outcome?

Force yourself to look beyond the moment at hand. In the heat of the moment, our tendency is to think only of *immediate* consequences, and our bias is to give more weight to data that pushes us in the direction that we are already leaning. Ask yourself:

- If I take this risk, what benefit might come tomorrow? A year from now? Five years from now? On my deathbed?
- What harm might come tomorrow? A year from now? Five years from now? On my deathbed?

We believe there is great danger in operating in secrecy. In his letter to the Ephesians, Paul urges us:

> Carefully determine what pleases the Lord. Take no part in the worthless deeds of evil and darkness; instead, expose them. It is shameful even to talk about the things that ungodly people do in secret. But their evil intentions will be exposed when the light shines on them, for the light makes everything visible. This is why it is said, "Awake, O sleeper, rise up from the dead, and Christ will give you light." (Eph. 5:10–14)

What can you do to make your own deeds visible? What if there were a hidden camera capturing your behavior, to be posted or broadcast for all the world to see? Would you be ashamed? What would become of your reputation? What would your spouse, children, parents, friends, and professional colleagues think? What would that do to your ability to continue performing your life's work effectively? Who else might get hurt or harmed when this becomes public? This line of self-inquiry will help you realistically assess the magnitude of risk in the decision you are contemplating and see the damage you might cause before it is done.

PART 3

CHAPTER 9

"THE GOLDEN BUZZER"

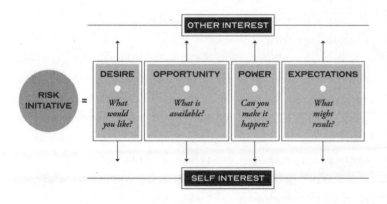

In 2006, a new talent search kicked off the summer TV season with *America's Got Talent*. Its creators sought to create a talent competition far grander than those of other televised talent contests. Since then, the "Got Talent" format has had more than

1 billion global viewers. From its inception, *America's Got Talent* has been the highest-rated and most watched summer television show, dominating the rest of its competition.

The show's format is fairly predictable. The program attracts a variety of participants, acts ranging from singing, to dancing, comedy, magic, stunts, variety, and more. Each participant who auditions attempts to secure a place in the live episodes of a season by impressing a panel of judges. Those that make it into the live episodes compete against each other for both the judges' and public's vote in order to reach the live final, where the winner receives a large cash prize and a chance to headline a show on the Las Vegas Strip.

In *AGT*'s ninth season, the show added a new format to the auditions in the form of the "Golden Buzzer." During auditions, each judge is allowed to use the Golden Buzzer to send an act automatically into the live shows, regardless of the opinion of the other judges. The purpose of the Golden Buzzer was to save an act from elimination by overriding the fellow judges "no" votes.

A *Newsweek* article describing all the contestants who have received the Golden Buzzer had this to say about a special performer in 2021:

> Judge Simon Cowell pressed his Golden Buzzer after getting emotional listening to "It's Okay," an original song by a thirty-year-old singer named Jane, who performs under the pseudonym Nightbirde. The performer also revealed

that she was battling cancer from which she had a "two percent chance of survival." She told the judges, "Last time I checked, I had some cancer in my lungs, spine and my liver. It's important that everyone knows I'm so much more than the bad things that happened to me." Cowell told *People Magazine*: "I was absolutely mesmerized. Every year we meet the most extraordinary people on this show. She's an amazing person with an incredible talent and she's truly an inspiration."[6]

While gold glitter falls from above and across the stage, the surprised and tearful recipient of the Golden Buzzer is greeted with a cheering and adoring crowd, hugs from the judges, and a free pass straight to the next round of competition. And though there is no guarantee that being awarded a Golden Buzzer will result in being declared the overall *AGT* winner, since its inception, five out of six *AGT* winners were Golden Buzzer recipients.

With every decision a leader makes and with every risk a leader takes, there will be winners and there will be losers. Unfortunately, there are no judges standing by to reward leaders with a Golden Buzzer that will save them from elimination due to a bad decision. However, we believe leaders have their very own Golden Buzzer, and when used thoughtfully it will save both leaders and their followers a great deal of heartache while simultaneously catapulting them closer to making good decisions.

• • •

The Golden Buzzer of risk-taking has saved us from a lot of grief around LCBC Church.

LCBC began in the garage of Don and Joyce Hershey. A group of thirty-five to forty people met together in a garage to pray for Don and Joyce's son—a sixteen-year-old who had been diagnosed with a brain tumor. Within months of praying together, this small band of people began to entertain the idea of starting a new church.

As they dreamed of forming a new church, they knew what kind of church they didn't want to be. They didn't want their new church to be like so many other churches they had attended. Instead, they dreamed of a church that would be different. Rather than being a church that was focused on meeting the needs of those already in the church, this group dreamed of forming a church that would be focused on the needs of *others*. Their dream was to start a church that would be focused on reaching out to others—others who were far from God.

The focus on others was significant to Don and Joyce Hershey. It was a focus that had changed Don's life. As a young man, Don was profoundly influenced by someone he had worked with at the Skicraft Boat Company. Though he was brought up in a religious tradition, Don didn't know he could have a personal relationship with Jesus until he met Ruben Miller.

While working the night shifts together at the Skicraft Boat Company, Ruben inspired Don to read the Bible. And it was while reading the Bible that Don first realized God loved him, wanted a personal relationship with him, and had a plan for his life. As they worked installing teak in the floors of boats, Don began to sense that there were others who needed to hear that Jesus loves them too.

So Don had a friend paint the word *Others* on a scrap of teak, and he took it home and put it over the kitchen door. Growing up, Don and Joyce's children said they would see the *Others* sign every time they went out the door and were reminded to think of others first. Other people who needed Jesus. Other people who needed to know that they are a top priority to Jesus.

Don and Joyce's family grew up realizing that they were representing God, and what they did and said had an impact on others. It was such a profound, but simple message. Late in life, when Don and Joyce were downsizing their home, they asked their two daughters what they might want to take from their home. Above all the treasures in Don and Joyce's home, (if you saw Don and Joyce's home, you would know there were many, many treasures to choose from), what both girls wanted most was Don's *Others* sign.

So, Don commissioned someone to reproduce that sign, and now each of the girls has her very own *Others* sign. They say that almost everyone who comes to visit notices the sign and asks about it. Don's daughter Doreen said that whenever she gets to feeling under-appreciated or discouraged, she's reminded by the sign, "It's not about me. And the best way to be useful to God is to help someone else."

> A focus on others rather than a focus on self is the Golden Buzzer of calculated risk-taking.

A focus on others rather than a focus on self is the Golden Buzzer of calculated risk-taking. And people follow leaders who are more concerned about others than about themselves.

• • •

In our first several years of marriage, Ruth and I loved to snow ski. Even though Texas has no ski slopes of its own, Texans brag that God created Colorado so Texans could go skiing.

Twice a year—once on Christmas night and then again over Spring Break—we would load up two chartered motor coaches full of high school and college students along with their leaders and embark on a grueling 24-hour bus ride from Dallas, Texas, to Colorado. Needless to say, having been deprived of a full night's sleep and now deprived of oxygen, emotions were on edge as our buses climbed 9,000 feet to the base of Mount Crested Butte.

The first day on the slopes was both exhilarating and terrifying. It is my belief that there is nothing like looking across the horizon while on the top of a 10,000-foot mountain, only to see a deep blue sky topping off the endless, snow-covered peaks of the Rockies. I was never really sure if it was the thin air, the cold, or the beauty of the mountains that would truly take my breath away.

The terror came as our "experienced and expert" skiers mistakenly convinced our "never before" skiers that they did not need lessons but instead would learn better by going directly to the top of the mountain. That was a lie. And by noon there would often be twenty to thirty novice skiers in tears, stranded on black diamond slopes, scattered across Mount Crested Butte, inching their way down by sliding on their bottoms.

Not surprisingly, by the second day, our "skied once before" skiers were more willing to consider lessons on the bunny slopes. That afternoon, after having taken lessons, I would lead a large group up the mountain while staying on green and eventually blue slopes for all to enjoy. As this comical, floundering mass of humanity would throw themselves down the slopes at varying speeds, I would ski slightly ahead and scout out the next best trail for the group to enjoy. By day three they were pairing up into threes and fours and venturing out on their own to enjoy and explore appropriate trails down the mountain.

What was the difference between day one and day two on the slopes? Well, besides acclimating to the thin mountain air and learning to stay upright and to snowplow, group members began to focus on others and not just on themselves.

On day one, our expert skiers not only wanted to prove and demonstrate their skills to the rest of the pack; they also wanted to ski on slopes that would be more challenging and rewarding for themselves. Little time was spent remembering their first moments on skis or what it was like to be frightened while doing something brand-new and dangerous. It never crossed their minds how humiliating and demoralizing it would be for these novice skiers to be left stranded on the side of a black diamond slope—let alone the possibility of injury. And day one would end with tears, frustration, doubt, fear, and accusations of harmful intent.

But by day two the focus had changed. Now the attention was on the novice skiers. Giving them a love of the mountain was paramount. And directing them down the mountain safely while sharing good experiences was a top priority. Day two would end with smiles, a sense of accomplishment, and a new confidence that is only gained by learning a new skill and conquering fears.

The difference between day one and day two was simply a focus on others. A focus on others is the Golden Buzzer for risk-taking. It doesn't guarantee a successful outcome, but it does bypass a lot of the pain and turmoil that come with self-focused decisions.

• • •

The idea of focusing on others is not original to Don Hershey. Nor is the idea of a church focusing on others original to LCBC. Focusing on others is an idea from God himself.

Hours before his death, Jesus said, "So now I am giving you a new commandment: Love each other. Just as I have loved you, you should love each other. Your love for one another will prove to the world that you are my disciples" (John 13:34–35).

The apostle Paul warned us not just to give lip service to this new command. "Don't just pretend to love others. Really love them. Hate what is wrong. Hold tightly to what is good. Love each other with genuine affection, and take delight in honoring each other" (Rom. 12:9–10).

Later, Paul challenges us to treat and love others as Jesus loved others—with humility and by putting others first:

> Don't be selfish; don't try to impress others. Be humble, thinking of others as better than yourselves. Don't look out only for your own interests, but take an interest in others, too. You must have the same attitude that Christ Jesus had. Though he was God, he did not think of equality with God as something to cling to. Instead, he gave up his divine privileges; he took the humble position of a slave and was born as a human being. When he appeared in human form, he humbled himself in obedience to God and died a criminal's death on a cross. (Phil. 2:3–8)

But here's the problem. Even though I know that I'm to put others first, I must admit it's often hard for me to do. My nature is to take care of myself first. My leaning is to grab all I can for myself, while simply letting others take care of themselves.

Putting others first in our risk-taking and decision-making means being more concerned about how it will affect them than about how it will affect me.

- Will making this move propel the church forward or propel me forward?
- Am I helping others mature in their walk with God or am I simply drawing a crowd around me?
- Will this ease my workload at the expense of adding to the loads of others?
- Will it make me look good or will the staff shine?
- Can I share the spotlight with others, or must I receive all the credit for this decision?
- Will it help accomplish our organizational goals over my personal goals?
- Will it prepare the organization for a better future or prepare me for my next move?
- Is this my decision, or is it our decision?
- If I take this risk, who stands to win—me or others?

• • •

Huge crowds were following Jesus. Perhaps they were interested in what Jesus had to say. Or maybe they simply came for the show, as Jesus was performing miracles by healing the sick. For whatever reason, the crowds kept coming and coming, and the group now swelled to over 5,000 men. Add in the women and children and the crowd was most likely pushing 15,000 people . . . 15,000 *hungry* people.

From the entire crowd, one boy steps forward. It's hard to imagine that he was the only person in a crowd this large that had planned ahead and brought a meal, but we do suspect he was the only one in the crowd who was willing to step forward and share his meal. After all, what would five barley loaves and two fish possibly help?

If others in the crowd held their food back, we wouldn't blame them. This would have been the perfect time to put into practice the old adage of "Do for one what you wish you could do for many"—and we would have been the ones enjoying the one meal. Fortunately, the crowd wasn't dependent on us!

But this boy steps up and willingly shares his meal with others. He's the hero. He put others first. We know, Jesus is the one who multiplied the bread and fish. And yes, if this boy didn't step forward, God could have provided some other way. But in this moment, no one else showed up—only a boy who was thinking about others first (John 6:1–15).

• • •

John Maxwell tells of a time when former congressman Bob McEwen had taken his four-year-old son for a burger and fries at the local McDonald's. As this father sat across from his son, watching him eat those fries ever so slowly, the dad began looking longingly at those fries, fries that began to look better and better, and more and more appetizing.

Finally, the dad reached across that table to grab a handful of those, fries that had been quietly calling his name. But as his dad reached, this four-year-old covered the fries with his hands and declared that these were *"my fries,"* and he didn't want his dad to have any of *"my fries."*

Well, the dad pulled his hand back and went into one of those rare dad-moments of deep thought and reflection. As he pondered, he came to the realization that his son did not understand where those fries had come from—what their source was. *I am the one who put down the money on the counter so that he could enjoy those fries in the first place. The only reason he had those fries at all was because of me—good ole Dad.*

Second, Dad thought, *I could reach over at any time and help myself to all of his fries! I could just grab any and all of "his fries" that I want!*

Finally, this dad concluded, *Not only does he not realize that I am the source of his French fries, or that I could take any or all of his fries that I want, but he also doesn't realize that I really don't need his fries, because I could go back over to that counter and buy my own bag of fries! I could even buy enough fries that I could bury my son in fries!*

Sometimes we forget, or maybe we just don't understand. God gives each and every one of us some French fries. He gives us talents, skills, intellect, resources, spiritual gifts, money. And he puts us in positions to lead. To some of us he gives a large bag of fries; to others he gives a small bag.

And once in a while he reaches down to our table for some fries. And he asks us to share some of those fries with others. Now, God doesn't need our fries; they are his to begin with. Yet we cover our bag and protect our bag of fries saying, "Hey, God, what are you doing reaching for my French fries? God, go get your own fries. Go take someone else's fries! Why would I want to share my fries with others? Let them get their own."

And like the dad at McDonald's, God is the owner, the giver of all our fries. You and I are simply the managers. And God asks us simply to share the fries we have with others. To put others first. And it must break the heart of God when we refuse to share some of his fries with others.

All that we have comes from God. So the question is: What are you doing with your fries? Are you willingly sharing the talents, the time, and the treasures God has given you with others? God provides us endless opportunities to impact others—if we choose not to ignore them.

The greatest differentiator in every decision a leader makes is their answer to the question, "Is this for me or for others?"

To be honest, at times, in the heat of the moment, it's hard to answer that question. After countless hours of immersing ourselves in the details—whether I'm making a choice that will be for my benefit or for others—the answer becomes foggy. And when forced to make a quick decision, it's not always clear who will be the greatest beneficiary.

But regardless of the clarity as we make our decisions, a successful end result of the risk initiative is dependent on whether we are self-focused or others-focused. In self-focused decisions we throw our hands around our French fries and we do all we can to preserve what we perceive to be ours. Self-focused decisions are about me, what I want, and what I think is best for me. Self-focused decisions are the antithesis of Jesus's decisions.

Others-focused decisions require humility. Others-focused decisions require putting others first. They require holding the needs of others before our own. But don't be confused. An others-focused life does not mean simply giving in to what others want. Instead, an others-focused life is choosing what is best for others over self. Jesus gave his life for others. Jesus lived the ultimate others-focused life.

● ● ●

But if an "others" focus is the Golden Buzzer of making good decisions and taking wise risks, there is an equally powerful force in play that at best will diminish the influence and impact of a leader and at worst derail a leader's ability to lead and serve others. It is the primary force that causes leaders to stumble and fall.

CHAPTER 10

WHEN LEADERS FALL

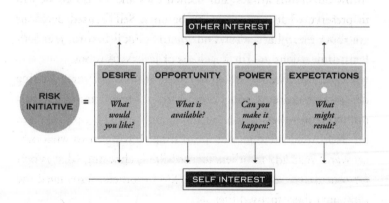

"*hat were you thinking?*"

This time, I (David) was the one asking the question. As I read the report, a sick feeling came over me—that sick feeling that rushes in when you hear something so troubling it surely can't be true. That sick feeling that comes with the realization that your world is about to change. It's that kick in the gut when you hear words you never wanted to hear.

I had heard stories like this before, but those stories were always about leaders I didn't know—leaders that I didn't hold with such high regard, who surely had obvious character flaws that caused them to stumble.

But this was different. This was someone I knew. This was someone I looked up to. This was someone I considered my mentor, even if only from a distance. This was someone who had helped shape and stretch my leadership skills. This was someone who had greatly influenced our church. And this was someone Ruth (my wife) and I had just spent the evening with not two weeks before, sitting out on the deck of his hotel suite, sharing stories and crackers and cheese with a few other friends and acquaintances.

My initial reaction after processing the full article was, *This can't be true! There must be some mistake—just a misunderstanding between friends and coworkers.* But over the following hours and then days the accusations increased. A pattern of poor behavior or—at the very least—a pattern of poor decision-making and unwise risk-taking came to light.

Because he had influenced and touched the lives of so many others, the news spread quickly across the country and around the globe. There was no thought of keeping this quiet. There was no hope that it would simply go away.

After a series of denials and rebuttals to the growing list of accusations, while speculation surrounding the leader's behavior continued to escalate, I watched sadly as my mentor—my *friend*—stepped away from his position of leadership.

And just like that, another leader fell.

The questions that have haunted me since are these: *How did this happen? How could such a great leader fall? What was he thinking?*

• • •

If we have any hope of living our lives to the fullest, we must learn to embrace risks. Our ability to manage risks well will determine whether or not we break away from a life of mediocrity. There is a danger in playing it too safe. But there is also a danger in embracing risks. Leaning into risk means living close to the edge, and the more we live and dance on the edge, the more we increase our potential to fall.

> The more we live and dance on the edge, the more we increase our potential to fall.

Film director Dennis Dugan (of *Happy Gilmore* fame) said, "In order to find the edge, you must risk going over the edge."[7] Taking risks requires that leaders live close to the edge. Which is an inherently dangerous place to live.

Living on the edge of risks means there is a fine line between taking wise risks and breaking ahead of the pack, and taking foolish risks and falling completely away from it. The more success a leader experiences while taking risks, the more he or she opens the door to becoming reckless in some of the most vulnerable aspects of their lives.

We see this played out while a person moves closer and closer to the edge of a cliff in an attempt to take the perfect photo. As their comfort level rises while being on the cliff's edge, so does their risk of falling. Perhaps they'll walk away with a photo like none other, but more and more we read in the news of the person who tragically fell to their death in their attempt to move one step closer to the edge.

Bottom line: there is a shadow side to embracing risks. Over time a leader grows comfortable living close to the edge, only to misstep and plunge to their demise. Having fallen, most often these leaders find themselves asking, *"What was I thinking?"*

• • •

Almost from the beginning of my tenure at LCBC Church, our official mission has been "to introduce more people to Jesus and together fully follow him." This is the statement that drives everything we do. With every decision we make, we hold each decision up against this statement, and we ask, "Will this decision truly help us introduce more people to Jesus and together more fully follow him?"

But there is a second statement that also impacts all we do. This statement has been around LCBC Church almost as long as the first, but you won't find it printed on our literature. You won't see it hung on banners around the church or written across our office walls. But we review it with all of our team on a regular basis.

Our unofficial mission statement says, "Let's not do any-thing stupid to mess up what God is doing." Stupid can be a lot of things. Stupid covers a lot of ground.

When we talk around LCBC about not doing stupid things to mess up what God is doing, it is our observation that most churches don't fail because of doctrinal or theological arguments or disagreements. Instead, most churches fail because church leaders make poor decisions, take foolish risks, dance too close to the edge. They run out of leadership coins and then go bankrupt.

Sadly, it is extremely difficult for both a church and that church's leader to recover when a leader falls. So, if the most common differentiator between taking a well calculated risk and a poor decision is the Golden Buzzer—an others-focus rather than a self-focus—what drives a leader to make poor choices and take foolish risks? What causes a leader to dance too close to the edge?

• • •

In his 1625 oil painting, Peter Paul Rubens portrayed the goddess Thetis dipping her son Achilles in the River Styx. As an infant, Achilles was dipped into the river by his mother in order to make him immortal. But since she held him by one heel, this spot did not touch the water, and so remained mortal and vulnerable. And it was here that Achilles eventually was mortally wounded.

Today, the tendon that stretches up the calf from the heel is called the Achilles' tendon. But the term Achilles' heel isn't used in medicine. It's used as a cliche with the general meaning "weak point." An Achilles' heel is a weakness in spite of overall strength, which can lead to unforeseen downfall.

Every leader has an Achilles' heel. And unless we can identify our weak points, we are destined to fail. Every leader is capable of doing stupid things and messing up what God is doing. And unless we are willing to admit our propensity to do stupid things, we are setting ourselves up to fail.

To avoid doing something stupid, we first must learn to recognize the shadow side of embracing risks. Success breeds pride and confidence. Time living on the edge dulls our senses to the dangers. Just ask the countless leaders who have fallen while living on the edge. Any leader who spends any time living on the edge is vulnerable! No one is immune. We all have our weaknesses. We are all capable of doing stupid things.

● ● ●

Acknowledging the reality that we all have an Achilles' heel, Pope Gregory the Great developed a growing concern over people's poor decisions that were destroying relationships with God and with others. So Gregory created a list of what he called the "seven deadly sins." He described them as seven deadly sins of passion—sins that were self-focused rather than others-focused. In his observation of the culture around him, Pope Gregory the Great found these seven deadly sins to be fueling an individual's drive and motivation in his or her decision-making, with disastrous results.

Interestingly, hundreds of years later we see these same seven deadly sins still very much at play in the choices we make and the risks we choose to take. (At LCBC we've actually found the seven deadly sins to make a great sermon series!) Pope Gregory's list includes: pride, envy, greed, lust, gluttony, anger, and slothfulness.

If an "others" focus is the Golden Buzzer of making good decisions and taking wise risks, we believe that the greatest of Pope Gregory's seven deadly sins is the "poisoned pill" of taking risks—none other than the sin of pride.

A quick glance at Scripture tells us that pride has been a destructive element throughout all of human history—which makes it all the more important that we call out and name the sin in order to heighten our awareness of what may be going on inside our heads and hearts as we make critical decisions. Pride is the excessive belief in our own abilities. Pride is thinking too highly of ourselves. Pride is me always wanting to be better than you.

The truth about pride (and actually all seven of the deadly sins) is that pride is probably present in your life right now. And your friends and family and all the people around you know you struggle with pride, but they will almost never tell. Why? Because even if they did, you wouldn't listen! You would just deny it. But your enemies—people who dislike you and do not believe in your leadership—are more than happy to tell you about this issue (and more) in your life! (Don't tell them this, but their eagerness to tell you about your pride might be due to their *own* pride. This deadly sin really doesn't discriminate . . .)

None of us wants to admit we struggle with pride. We wholeheartedly believe everyone else struggles with it, but somehow we don't think we do. Somehow you think that you are immune to pride—but you're not. Pride in you and in me is real, and it damages our relationships and causes us to make poor decisions and to take foolish risks.

Don Shula, the legendary former coach of the Miami Dolphins, told a story about being on vacation with his wife in Maine, when they walked into a movie theater. There was just a handful of people there, and when Shula and his wife walked in, the people applauded. Shula said he was pretty pleased with himself—noting that he was famous even in Maine. He nudged his wife and said, "I guess there is no place that we can go where I am not known."

Just before the movie started, a guy came over and shook his hand. Shula said to the man, "I'm surprised you folks know me here in Maine." The guy's response was, "Am I supposed to know you? We were just glad you came in. You, see the manager said he wasn't going to start the movie until there were at least ten people in here."[8]

Pride lives within every one of us. And pride causes a leader to take unnecessary and foolish risks. It's pride that keeps a leader from seeking or even listening to wise counsel. It's pride that blinds a leader from seeing the true facts involved in a critical decision. It's pride that causes a leader to make a choice that ends in humiliation rather than success.

> Pride causes a leader to take unnecessary and foolish risks.

Not many of us can tolerate a pride-filled person for long. They grate on us. They repel us. And what we learn from the Bible is that God feels the same way about pride as we do, but even more so. Here is some of what the Bible has to say about pride:

- "Pride leads to conflict; those who take advice are wise" (Prov. 13:10).
- "Pride goes before destruction, and haughtiness before a fall" (Prov. 16:18).
- "Better to live humbly with the poor than to share plunder with the proud" (Prov. 16:19).
- "Pride ends in humiliation, while humility brings honor" (Prov. 29:23).

- "God opposes the proud but favors the humble" (James 4:6).

That last one ought to keep every leader up at night. God sets himself against the proud. God opposes the proud. We can think of many human forces in this world we would not want opposing us. We wouldn't want LeBron James opposing us on a basketball court. We wouldn't want Stone Cold Steve Austin or The Undertaker opposing us in a wrestling ring. We wouldn't want Bill Gates opposing us at an auction. We wouldn't want Tom Brady opposing us in the Super Bowl. But even more, *we wouldn't want the almighty God opposing every step of our paths.* But that's how much God resists the agenda of arrogant people.

God opposes the proud but favors the humble. Think about it. What would it be like for the sovereign God of the universe to stand directly in front of you with his arms crossed and say, *"I will oppose your plans. I will oppose your agenda. I will oppose the path you're walking on. And I will oppose you because of your arrogance."*

Martin Luther called pride "the deepest of all human vices." If you search the Bible for the one sin that most incites the wrath of God, it's pride. One writer said that the one sin that moves God to corrective action almost every single time is arrogance. God can't stand it. And there is no greater or more foolish risk than making decisions rooted in pride and an over-inflated ego.

> Though the LORD is great, he cares for the humble, but he keeps his distance from the proud. (Ps. 138:6)

Because pride impacts our relationships, what we have discovered is that when our relationships are off—when there is chaos, discord, alienation at work or at home, when we find ourselves feeling distant from God or from loved ones—it's usually not everyone else that's the problem. More often than not, I am the one who has the problem. Often that problem is pride.

A strong caution light that pride is rearing its ugly head in our lives is a lack of peace with those around us. And when we're not at peace with those who are closest to us—our spouse, our best friends, our leadership team—we have learned that it's not wise to move forward with questionable risks or decisions.

• • •

Over time, leaders learn they must take calculated risks. However, following years and years of successfully tackling calculated risks, leaders grow in their comfort with risks, including even foolish or reckless risks. Dangerously, leaders inflate their ability to handle risks. Unfortunately, the line between self-confidence and pride is very fine.

When a person achieves success while taking risks, they develop the belief that they will be successful taking *all* risks. So, one's Achilles' heel of pride grows out of the notoriety that comes with being successful in the face of risk.

Individuals who have proven to be successful in taking risks often receive elevated status from their peers. Status is reputational; it refers to the respect and prestige one has in the eyes of others. High-status individuals enjoy more freedom to make decisions and act on them.

Because of a newly elevated status and additional freedom, a successful leader is given a longer leash by which to operate. Unfortunately, when successful leaders are handed a longer rope to operate—often it becomes just enough rope by which they hang themselves while taking a foolish risk.

Blinded by the light of their successes, they believe their successes are due to personal rather than external or divine causes. This in turn causes a leader to think that because they have been successful facing risk in one area of their life, they are now destined to succeed with taking risks in all areas of life.

• • •

While driving down the Pennsylvania Turnpike, a four-lane-highway with two lanes going east and two lanes going west, I (David) encountered a high level of traffic and congestion. My cruise-control was appropriately set at 79 mph for the 70 mph speed limit. In spite of the heavy amount of cars on the road, we were able to move along at a pretty good clip.

As I moved in and out of the passing lane, I came upon a long line of cars following a slower truck in the right-hand lane. I moved back into the passing lane, which was clear as far as I could see in front of me, and as long as the other eight or ten slower cars stayed in the right-hand lane behind the truck, all would be well. But I could sense some of these drivers were getting antsy. I just knew someone was going to pull out in front of me, forcing me to slow down and disrupt my journey. *Don't do it! Don't do it! Don't you dare do it!* I repeated in my head. *Don't even think about it. Stay in your lane!*

I've found that sometimes slower drivers pull out of their lane on purpose. It's as though they feel entitled to the entire road. Other times it's out of stupidity. They're just oblivious to the other cars and drivers around them. Then there are times it happens accidently, as a driver gets lazy and simply drifts across the line. Whatever the reason, it's in these moments that I wish I could get into the minds of these other drivers and whisper (or shout), *Stay in your lane!*

When they do choose to pull out into the passing lane, at best it's a disruption to those of us already in that lane. But at its worst, it might lead to an accident that could lead to injury or great harm, maybe even death.

Like drivers on the Pennsylvania Turnpike, pride causes leaders to carelessly pull out of their lane and at best disrupt those around them, but at worst cause harm or great pain to those in their sphere of influence.

For instance, because of our extensive training and experiencing success while taking a risk in becoming a communicator of God's Word, pastors are tempted to believe that we are equally qualified to take the risk of giving advice about managing finances, or how to vote, or how to run a business or lead a school.

As a young pastor in my late twenties, I fell into this trap, believing that I could save the marriage of some close friends who were twice my age. With nothing but an introductory counseling course in seminary, for an entire year, after wrapping up my responsibilities of leading something we used to call Wednesday evening prayer meetings, I would go and spend the rest of the evening at the home of my friends in an attempt to "save" their marriage.

Weekly, I would listen to my friends put each other down or flat-out ignore each other, or at times scream and yell at each other, all because I thought I was qualified to function as their marriage counselor. I believed I was more than qualified because I had experienced success as a Bible teacher to newly married young couples, and as a leader who revived and re-energized a dying children's camp. Therefore, in my mind, of course I was qualified to be a marriage counselor.

These weekly sessions ended with little to no improvement in the marriage and concluded when I moved from Dallas to Lancaster, Pennsylvania. However, buoyed by my new role as a first-time senior pastor, I picked right back up where I had left off. Once again, I was convinced a struggling couple needed my help. Once again, I listened to them put each other down, or flat-out ignore each other, or at times scream and yell at each other. Once again, there was little or no evidence of any improvement in this marriage.

And it was at that point that I became painfully aware of the fact that I had taken a risk and stepped into an area that was beyond my experience or training or expertise. I had gotten out of my lane. I wrongly assumed that because I had experienced success as a teacher and a leader, I would also experience success as a counselor. But I failed miserably. Not only was I not a good counselor; I most likely only added to the problems these two couples were facing. I should have stayed in my lane.

Experiencing success while taking risks can be deceiving because it fools us into believing we are qualified to take risks in all areas of life. As leaders, we get ourselves into trouble when we begin taking risks outside of our areas of expertise.

As a result of my failed attempts at marriage counseling, I determined that it would be prudent for me to stay in my lane as a pastor and only do what I could do well as a pastor. We also adopted that philosophy as a church, focusing only on what we could do well as a church. Rather than serving our people poorly, we began to outsource areas of need that were beyond our strengths to experts in our community.

As a new need or opportunity presented itself to our church, we would remind ourselves: "We are a church, not a counseling center. We are a church, not a school. We are a church, not a food kitchen. We are a church and not qualified to solve world hunger." And we began resourcing schools and food kitchens and other organizations who were already serving our community well.

You may not be a pastor, and your organization may not be a church, but you too have areas of giftedness and expertise. But don't assume your past successes with risk automatically translate into future successes. Figure out where you are strong as well as where you are weak; then trust others with what others can do better. Leaders fall because of inflated levels of self-confidence.

George Herbert Walker Bush, the 41st president of the United States, left a legacy of colorful quotes that his followers loved, and his critics exploited. I (David) adopted one such quote and used it again and again with my then teenage children. When they would ask permission to do something questionable, I would channel my best George H. W. Bush impersonation and reply, "It wouldn't be prudent." But as you might imagine, this response did not typically go over well with my kids!

So reaching back a few years and channeling my best George H. W. Bush impersonation, let me say, "It wouldn't be prudent" to simply assume that because you've been successful with risk in one area of your life you will automatically be successful with risks in all areas of your life. Let me take it one step further. Not only would it not be prudent to assume you can be successful with all risks, but it might even prove to be dangerous. (My hope is you receive this challenge better than my kids!)

• • •

Add selfishness to an inflated sense of self-importance and it produces an ugly spirit of entitlement. A sense of entitlement sets a leader up to fail while taking foolish risks. Especially vulnerable to a sense of entitlement are leaders in ministry who are overworked—who may not be fully appreciated, who are underpaid, and who feel they deserve to be treated better! Armed with feelings of entitlement, our perspective on what we deserve becomes skewed.

Because we are industrious, we begin to find ways to make up for our less than adequate salary. Because we know that what we do matters even when others don't notice, we take appreciation for our work wherever we can find it and from whoever is willing to give it.

As leaders we take risks, and with those risks we take on a great weight of responsibility that comes from putting our neck on the line again and again. Because we carry a weight or a burden that others don't, we begin to think we are entitled to favors and benefits others aren't—because, after all, we are the only ones who truly understand the weight of putting our necks on the line again and again.

That sense of entitlement causes us to feel as though normal rules and procedures (boundaries meant to protect us from foolish decisions) no longer apply to us. These rules and procedures are for others—those who don't carry the same burden or weight that we do, who aren't as underappreciated as we are. Unwittingly we fall into a cycle that builds and grows until we begin to make foolish and overly risky decisions in all areas of life.

This cycle of entitlement is fairly predictable. We take a risk, which leads to a sense of entitlement. Feeling entitled, we begin to believe that rules are meant for others, but surely they don't apply to us. Now free from rules and restrictions, more risks can be taken. As more risks are taken, the weight of those risks increases, which leads to more feelings of entitlement, which lead to more rules that don't apply to us, which allows for more risk-taking, which eventually results in a foolish decision.

Amazingly, when we fall having made a foolish decision, it's those same feelings of entitlement that causes us to shake our fists at God. We complain and blame God as though it's his fault for letting this happen to us. After all, we fell while sacrificing and serving him so faithfully! But Proverbs 19:3 (NIV) tells us, "A person's own folly leads to their ruin, yet their heart rages against the LORD." We make the foolish decision, and we blame God for not blessing it.

Not only do we carry the extra weight of responsibility, but as leaders we are also constantly confronted with criticism for our decisions. Therefore, in order to push forward and defy the odds, we dismiss our naysayers. Unfortunately, this also leads us to dismiss wise, constructive criticism. Rather than listen to even the most trusted voices around us, we simply withdraw from all people in order to protect ourselves from unwanted comments. Before long, we find ourselves living and operating in isolation.

Combating this tendency to take on risks in isolation, Solomon said, "Plans go wrong for lack of advice; many advisers bring success" (Prov. 15:22) and, "Don't go to war without wise guidance; victory depends on having many advisors" (Prov. 24:6).

Taking risks in isolation is reckless. Whether we are taking personal risks or professional risks, when we take a risk that we wouldn't want anyone else to know about or comment on, there's a strong chance that we've become reckless in our decisions. But, if we are not afraid of sharing or telling others about those risks, it's safe to say we are probably making good decisions or at least are willing to be protected from making bad ones.

Warning signs are all around us, telling us to slow down, maybe even to turn back. These signs might pop up in a lack of peace or rattled nerves or disrupted sleep. Ignoring them sets us up for a fall.

The most obvious warning signs come through the voices of those around us—a board member, coworkers, a spouse, a good friend. But as a leader grows in status and success, those around them are more reluctant to willingly share their true thoughts and concerns. Those closest to a leader are often fearful of confronting or being truthful. "What if my concerns are wrong? What if my objections are not well received? Why risk being humiliated by that leader?"

But the true thoughts and feelings of a trusted friend, coworker, or board member are exactly what a successful leader needs to hear. The reality is that the more successful you are as a leader, the more you need to ask others to question you and to call you out.

Frequently, a leader is so immersed in the culture of the organization and so wrapped up in the details of the situation that they are unaware of the present dangers and threats to the organization. A leader who is too comfortable in his surroundings often becomes "nose-blind" to their organization.

> The more successful you are as a leader, the more you need to ask others to question you and to call you out.

To be *nose-blind* is to be oblivious to the smells in our home. To be "nose-blind" is to be unaware what our own home really smells like. It could be the smell of cat pee, garlic, or dirty socks. When someone is "nose-blind," they need someone else to point out what their home really smells like.

To be *nose-blind* in an organization means that it is often those on the outside of the organization who are quicker to recognize what is not right inside the organization. It is often easier to identify from the outside the warning signs that tell an organization it's about to crash and burn than it is for those on the inside who are too close to see what is really going on.

• • •

How tragic it is when leaders fall. How tragic it is when leaders do stupid things and thus mess up what God is doing. The apostle Paul said it well: "So be careful how you live. Don't live like fools, but like those who are wise. Make the most of every opportunity in these evil days. Don't act thoughtlessly, but understand what the Lord wants you to do" (Eph. 5:15–17).

I will never forget the moment as Ruth and I watched my friend and mentor address his congregation for the very last time. It was one of the most heartbreaking and deflating endings I have ever seen.

Final addresses are meant to be a tribute, a celebration of a life well lived and an organization well led. But after pouring most of his adult life into this organization, rather than ending his career by being honored and revered for all the good he had done, he walked off the platform one last time. No celebration. No honor. Only humiliation. Only disbelief.

In spite of all of this I still consider him to be my friend and mentor. And I am so thankful for the influence he has had on my life. But my heart aches both for him and for all who have been impacted by the fallout of his situation. And I hold firm to the hope that God is able to make something good out of broken vessels. All broken vessels.

CHAPTER 11

"I WAS THINKIN' 'BOUT A LITTLE WHITE TANK TOP"

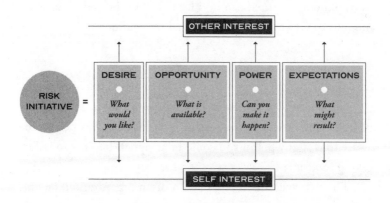

I (David) enjoy a good country song. Not only do I love the sound of a pedal steel guitar, I also appreciate the honesty of the story that's told in a good country song. For instance, singer

Dierks Bentley tells the story of a young man taking a risk by meeting up late one evening with a farmer's daughter.

Foolishly ignoring the wrath of an irate and protective father in order to experience the pleasure of being with his daughter, he later asks the question, *"What was I thinking?"*

Immediately he answers his own question by admitting that the only thing on his mind, and the only thing driving his foolish decision, was the girl in "the little white tank top" sitting in the car next to him.

A girl. A daddy. A shotgun. *"What was I thinking?"*

As the great theologian Forrest Gump once said, "Stupid is as stupid does." Stupid can be a lot of things. Stupid covers a lot of ground. Often, it involves a sexual temptation.

• • •

No matter who you are or how long you have been a follower of Jesus Christ or how "successful" you may be, you need to be aware that at any point, you could be tempted. It's easy to fall by taking foolish risks.

The damage caused to a church or an organization, or simply your own life, by a falling to the temptation to stray sexually is overwhelming and difficult to measure fully. Solomon tells us that sex outside of God's boundaries for sex will cost a man everything he has. No place is this more evident than for the man or woman who strays sexually while working in vocational ministry.

If married, the one who strays sexually risks losing their marriage and irreparably damaging their children. But for the fallen leader in full-time ministry, it goes beyond the family. There is a very strong likelihood that the one who strays sexually not only risks losing his or her family, but that the door of opportunity to continue leading will close, maybe permanently. An entire career and life's work is lost.

Sex outside of marriage will likely cost the one who strays everything. And it involves a risk like no other.

The causes of sexual affairs are endless: unmet needs; unfulfilled expectations; low self-esteem; on-going conflict; and uncontrolled thoughts, to name a few.

But making a wise and calculated decision about the risk of straying sexually goes much further than knowing the reasons a person might stray. The writer of the book of Hebrews (11:25) reminds us of what we know to be true from our

> There is pleasure in sin for a season, but that pleasure does not last.

own experiences. And that is that there is pleasure in sin for a season, but that pleasure does not last. So it's important to factor in the cost. What might result? "Immediate excitement and bliss, and also, most likely, total annihilation of all that I know."

We like the straightforward advice given by Dr. Joyce Brothers, who said, "I think we should follow a simple rule: if we can take the worst, take the risk."[9]

Driven by feelings and hormones and loaded with excuses as to why a sexual encounter outside of marriage is not only appropriate but also deserved, little thought is usually given to the cost of such an encounter. In our minds the four propositions of risk are all aligning, unchecked by any meaningful instruments of exposure or accountability, toward commission of sexual sin.

Therefore, we must magnify the consequences and minimize the benefits of taking sexual risks. These foolish risks will most likely result in a broken marriage, a crippled family, loss of income to support that struggling family, loss of a rewarding career leading and serving others, and a loss of influence with others, to name a few consequences. When we take these things into account, we will begin to protect ourselves on the front end from situations where we might become vulnerable to sexual sin.

As you are tempted to stray, your last line of defense against foolish risk lies with the expectations proposition, *What might result?* It is critical to consider carefully the impact and the results that the sexual gratification you are contemplating might have on important aspects of your life.

• • •

There are preventative measures we ought to be taking as leaders, and these measures are pretty obvious and straightforward. And yet we watch leaders fall again and again. So while running the risk of being redundant, let us suggest a few preventative measures:

- *Take the option of sex outside of marriage off the table.* Delete this option from the menu. Make a commitment to experience the joy of sex in marriage only. As the writer of Proverbs reminds us, "Drink water from your own well—share your love only with your wife" (5:15). "Let your wife be a fountain of blessing for you. Rejoice in the wife of your youth" (5:18). "Let her breasts satisfy you always. May you always be captivated by her love" (5:19).

- *Minimize the opportunities for foolish mistakes.* Be aware of what kinds of situations tempt you; then, avoid those situations. When you feel you are in a situation that is too hot, pray, right there on the spot, ask God to help you, and then immediately move away from that opportunity.

- *Establish boundaries and stick with them.* At LCBC we have very clear and defined boundaries for our staff. Men and women on our staff do not travel, eat meals, or meet in offices behind closed doors alone. As an organization, we actively impose those constraints on our staff. It's not a matter of trust; it's simply recognizing and acknowledging the power of temptation. Prudish or not, we are committed to our unwritten mission statement of not doing anything stupid to mess up what God is doing at LCBC—even if it means giving up some personal rights or creating tighter boundaries for ourselves.

- *Don't give in to flattering speech.* We all tend to be susceptible to someone of the opposite sex who affirms and flatters us, so be careful. Proverbs 7:21–23 describes the folly of one who listens to flattering speech: "So she seduced him with her pretty speech and enticed him with her flattery. He followed her at once, like an ox going to the slaughter. He was like a stag caught in a trap, awaiting the arrow that would pierce its heart. He was like a bird flying into a snare, little knowing it would cost him his life."

These strategies aren't new, nor are they earth shattering—you already knew them. But too often we still play with fire. We overestimate our strength and underestimate our vulnerability. We overestimate the odds of a positive outcome and underestimate the odds of a dire impact to ourselves and our loved ones. We try to see just how close to the fire we can get without getting burned—just toying with the ideas until we are swept in and over our heads.

• • •

All my life I (David) had assumed all pastors were like my dad—honest, upright, godly men who also happen to be excellent leaders. That's why I was so taken aback when I first caught wind of Pastor Billy Weber's fall. Billy Weber had been the pastor of one of the fastest-growing churches in the Southern Baptist Convention. By forty-five years of age, Billy Weber had been cemented as one of the brightest stars in Baptist circles. He was a powerful preacher and a strong leader, and in 1977 had started Prestonwood Baptist Church in Dallas, Texas, with a handful of members that grew to more than 11,000 some ten years later.

Apparently, I wasn't the only one surprised by Billy Weber's fall. In late September of 1988, Prestonwood church leaders sat stunned and in disbelief when they found out that the rumors were true—Weber had had an affair with a married woman who was active in the church. One of the longtime deacons was quoted in an article in *D Magazine*: "It was a horrible experience." "They'd watched other church leaders fall from grace one by one," said the article's author. "Now the humiliation was theirs." Further investigation found that Weber had a pattern of infidelity. During his years at Prestonwood, he had as many as ten affairs, sometimes with several women simultaneously.

In a July 1989 article entitled "The Second Coming of Billy Weber," *D Magazine* summed it up this way:

The pattern of adultery points to a man who came to believe that the rules no longer applied to him, that what he was preaching on Sunday was meant for those in the pews, not the man in the pulpit. With the benefit of hindsight, some church leaders are beginning to see how they were used. Answerable to no one, Weber built a world of wealth and power where he hobnobbed with celebrities . . . he led the life of a corporate prince, and saw multiple loves as his just reward.[10]

Concerning his fall, Weber himself said maybe it happened, "because I am just a man who allowed himself to become physically exhausted and therefore spiritually exhausted. Maybe Satan targeted me at a time when our church was moving even more aggressively to find those who were lost and bring them into the family of faith and hope. . . . A persons' strength often becomes a weakness in that the more sensitive you become, the more vulnerable you are."[11]

William Tolar, then president of Southwestern Baptist Seminary, said, "It happened through a series of rationalizations. Sometimes we see this in rising young stars. They feel they are the exceptions, that the rules don't really apply to them. There's a subtle, subtle type of rationalization that goes on. But for a minister to do it again and again, he's developed a pattern of egotism. It boggles my mind."[12]

This was the first time I can remember asking myself, *How did this happen? How could this happen to anyone—but especially to him? He's such a great leader!*

CHAPTER 12

PUTTING THE DOPE MODEL TO THE TEST

By now you have a deep appreciation for how the four propositions work together in your own approach to risk-based decisions. You have also learned the critical role of self-other-interest, the differentiator between good and bad risk-based decisions. The figure below illustrates how self-other-interest bears upon risk initiative.

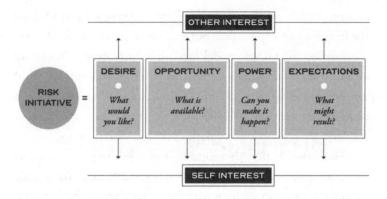

Here you will see that each of the four propositions—desire, opportunity, power, and expectations—is tied to a continuous and fluctuating tension that bears upon the propositions as a function of self-interest or other-interest, the differentiator that can point you toward the bright or dark side in your risk-based decisions.

Other-interested behavior generally functions as a levitating force, in that to the extent we press toward loving and serving others, we minimize any proneness to destructive or foolish risks. Self-interested behavior, on the other hand, is a gravitating force that drags us down, distracts us from what is right and good, and tempts us toward dysfunctional responses to the four propositions.

If we were able to animate the figure above, you would see the arrows bouncing and stretching up and down across the propositions, as we are in a constant state of flux, managing the tension that arises as we make decisions and take risks to advance the kingdom and to muddle our way through day-to-day living.

Putting the DOPE model to work is fairly simple. While we do not offer a *formula* to *guarantee* that every risk you take will pay healthy dividends, DOPE offers a *process* that, if practiced consistently, will lead to a life well-lived and pleasing to God—one that is characterized by both faith and wise restraint.

First, realize that the same four propositions of risk come into play with any risk-based decision you might face. You simply cannot escape confrontation with these propositions, but you can consciously manage the way you process them:

> **Desire:** "What would you like?"
>
> **Opportunity:** "What is available?"
>
> **Power:** "Can you make it happen?"
>
> **Expectations:** "What might result?"

If you wish to be consistent in making good decisions and taking healthy risks, you must first learn to navigate your way through each of the four propositions. That starts by carefully considering and then writing out your responses to each one, keeping in mind the various recommendations we have offered throughout chapters 5–8 for addressing desire, opportunity, power, and expectations.

• • •

Let's put the DOPE Model to work. While the DOPE Model was constructed for leaders and with leadership decisions and risks in mind, we could pick any number of life's decisions to put through the DOPE Model and find it helpful in calculating risks in most every situation.

So, let's put the DOPE Model into practice by analyzing a decision that every leader has faced more than once in life. Let's look at the risks that are involved in a decision to move into a new role with a new organization.

Risk = new job

To make a good decision and take a wise and calculated risk, we must first examine the four propositions. Remember, a proposition is an invitation to step into the risk. It's a call or suggestion or enticement to come and partake in the risk—in our case, a new job.

To truly put the DOPE Model to the test, let's look at a real scenario that David faced over fifteen years ago.

TEST CASE

LCBC Church had grown from 150 to 6,000 attendees in one location, and once again we were out of space. To use our space fully meant offering four weekend gatherings, two on

Saturday evening and two on Sunday morning. At the time I was the primary teacher, teaching four times per week, forty or so weeks a year, and I was emotionally tired. Expanding our facilities would require a campaign to raise the necessary funds to build, which is always exhausting. More growth required hiring more staff. But most of all, not expanding meant stagnation, and I am not a good maintainer; I am motivated by mission and challenge.

When I first took the role as Senior Pastor at LCBC, I promised God that as long as I was at LCBC I would not go looking for any other jobs. Time and time again I had watched pastors move from church to church. Each time ministry became hard and tension in the church was high, pastors would start looking for the next church to lead. Miraculously, God always seemed to "call" them to a location with warmer weather and sunnier skies. I was determined not to be one of those pastors.

Then I received a package in the mail, inviting me to consider making a vocational move. The open role was for the senior leadership position with a reputable international organization. The invitation was enticing, to say the least!

Proposition #1: What would you like?

Desire encompasses wants and cravings, and this new opportunity fed my appetite for responsibilities that would allow me to thrive and lead. It included things I desired, like influencing others, growing and expanding the organization's reach and impact, hiring and building a new team, casting vision for a preferable future, and representing the organization nationally as the senior leader.

But on the flip side, perhaps it was just boredom that attracted me to this new role. After fifteen years at LCBC, something new sounded fresh and exciting. Or maybe it was exhaustion: I was tired and needed rest. The fact that I was being pursued stroked my pride and ego. After all, what leader doesn't long to be wanted, to have more influence, more stature, and to make a greater impact?

Proposition #2: What is available?

Opportunity is about the circumstances that create potential to advance our desires. When the package containing this job offer arrived in the mail, so did the opportunity to meet my desires in a new and fresh way. This came out of the blue. I wasn't looking for it or expecting it. It simply added something to "here's what's available" that hadn't been there before. There was a new risk for me to consider that had never even been on my radar. Maybe God was placing this opportunity in front of me so I could serve him in a new way. And because I was tired and wondering whether my time at LCBC was done, the circumstances around me made me ripe for change.

But what I had so far neglected to do was generate more options. I allowed myself to get stuck thinking that my only options with respect to LCBC were to keep plugging along as we had been doing or to leave for greener pastures. Because I wasn't at a strong spot emotionally, I could not see that there was more to remaining at LCBC than my negative filter allowed me to see. I was aware that my fatigue was influencing my outlook, but underestimated just how much it was limiting my ability to see the possibilities. And I had not yet invited anyone else into the mix to help me evaluate my "duh" options or attempt to devise or see new ones.

Proposition #3: Can you make it happen?

Power is a person's capacity to make a difference in some measurable way. And based on my experience and skill set, this new position seemed tailor-made for me. And then there was the fact that I had been invited to apply. That suggested to me that the board of this organization already viewed me as a pretty strong candidate—they were already convinced I had something valuable to offer.

So, could I make the move to leadership in this new organization? They seemed to think so, and so did I. Not only did I have the ability to make the change being requested, I also believed I could thrive in this new position.

Looking back, it's evident that my mistake at that point was that I still wasn't applying the proposition "Can you make it happen?" to other options at LCBC. I wasn't considering what was still within my power to do where I already was.

Proposition #4: What might result?

Expectations are the anticipated possible outcomes should we choose to act. And there was nothing negative in my expectations should I make this move. In my estimation, because I'd been successful at LCBC, surely I would be successful again in this new organization. More people would be introduced to Jesus, and I would be allowed to lead and thrive in a new challenge.

At least that's what I assumed at the time. But if I'm truly honest with myself, I know that much of the success LCBC experienced over the years was due to other people and to factors beyond my influence or control, beyond my leadership. And that this new opportunity was different enough from leading a church in Lancaster County that I might not succeed.

In hindsight, it seems likely that my expectations of "What might result?" were too rosy. After all, I would be working under a board that I had no role in selecting or developing. I would be relying on team members I had no history with. I would be operating in regions and cultures—with accompanying sets of customs, politics, ethnic tensions, and business practices—that were foreign to me. To assume I would be successful in all those new challenges, where my leadership really hadn't been tested, was at best naivete, and at worst, pure hubris.

Introductions were made to the search team, interviews were conducted, and everything pointed to moving into this new role. It was time to see if this risk qualified for the Golden Buzzer!

Other-Interest or Self-Interest

The Golden Buzzer is awarded to decisions and risks that are focused on others rather than on ourselves. To be honest, I hadn't given the object of my decision much attention. I assumed that I had the interest of others as my top priority, but I had assumed incorrectly. In reality, I was enjoying being courted by a new organization. My sense of value and self-esteem were being stroked in a positive way. It was nice to be wanted!

My self-interest didn't come to light until I brought Ruth into the decision-making process. As we have previously stated, it is always prudent to seek outside advice when taking risks. But because of the nature of this decision, I had been moving forward while very much alone. I didn't feel I could discuss this with our church board, my closest friends were church members, and I was pretty sure Ruth would not initially respond well! My lack of transparency should have been a strong warning for me to slow down.

About this same time, I had undergone extensive knee surgery. Thus I was medicated throughout much of the interview process. Ruth was convinced my thoughts and interest in this job were drug-induced! And she might have been correct. A quick glance at the labels on any of my prescription bottles would have told me I was not in a good frame of mind to be making life-altering decisions!

What Ruth made clear to me was that while a job change might appear exciting to me, my thoughts were not in the best interest of LCBC. I needed that external perspective and should have sought it sooner. As I was confronting the four propositions of risk, I was trying to manage this big decision in isolation and from a mindset of fatigue. I was wrestling with my *own* thoughts and answering to *myself,* but I had not exposed my thinking to others nor invited them to push into the decision with me.

LCBC was at a crossroads. It would either keep moving forward or stand still. And, Ruth pointed out, all the things that attracted me to this new role were being fulfilled in my current role at LCBC. My leadership was needed to cast a new vision for the future, to grow and expand our reach, to influence others, to hire and build our ever-expanding team, and to continue to serve as the senior leader.

After more interviews—but now with Ruth involved and after calculating the risks—together we came to the conclusion that God was not leading us away from LCBC. Though I occasionally wonder what life would be like had I taken that position, looking back I am so thankful God allowed us to stay at LCBC. We would have missed so much.

It was at this crossroads that LCBC moved to multiple locations. Hundreds of new staff members were added, and LCBC's influence and reach was greatly expanded.

I had two great opportunities. I believe that I could have fully honored God through either choice. Neither was morally superior to the other. At the time, I couldn't know for sure how either would turn out. Each choice had its own set of risks. Had I chosen differently, maybe both organizations would be better than they are today, or maybe worse. But I'm not sweating what might or might not have been.

• • •

What decision are you now contemplating? What risk are you considering? Before jumping in head first, take time to examine the situation by allowing the DOPE Model to guide you as you calculate your risks. And don't forget about the Golden Buzzer!

TOOLS FOR ASSESSING AND MANAGING RISK

We have offered recommendations throughout this book to help you confront the four propositions effectively. Things like adopting the voice of a cynic to keep your desires (and fears) in check, setting boundaries that help you avoid unhealthy opportunities, actively inviting limitations on your power through reporting to a board or colleague, and posing questions like "What's the best that can happen?," "What are the real odds?," and "What if everybody knew?" as means of managing the expectations proposition.

Virtually all of our recommendations are designed to invite both exposure and accountability around the four propositions. Our recommendations are tools or instruments to help you navigate each of the four propositions successfully. Some must be self-imposed while others may be externally imposed or invited (sought by you from others).

Any such instrument that is self-applied and invites exposure is a matter of *self-awareness*—a means of *revealing something to yourself.* These include various questions you might ask yourself in order to gain an honest and accurate assessment of where you stand with respect to desire, opportunity, power, and expectations in any given situation. Self-awareness is a prerequisite to effective self-management.

Any instrument that is self-applied and invites accountability is a matter of *self-discipline*—a means of *answering to yourself.* These are the things you must train yourself to do or avoid doing, and they include various habits, boundaries, and practices that are useful to that end.

Any instrument that is externally applied and invites exposure is a matter of *transparency*—a means of *revealing to others* your thoughts and behaviors with respect to the four propositions. These kinds of interventions are designed to prevent you from operating in secret or in hiding. They are externally based (by imposition or invitation) means of shedding light on the risk-based decision under consideration. They expose you to other sets of eyes beyond your own, to help bring more scrutiny as you confront the four propositions of risk. Those other eyes will see things you are unable to see in yourself and your situation.

And any instrument that is externally applied and invites accountability is a matter of *audit*—a means of *answering to others* and providing techniques for monitoring you or protecting you from your own sin. We realize that on the face of it, that sounds pretty horrible and oppressive. But when the stakes are high and your actions have the potential to drag down a church or a company or otherwise harm lots of people, these types of external monitoring are necessary.

Many people are prone to seeing audits as suitable and necessary only to dire situations. So audits are typically implemented *after* some disastrous situation unfolds. *After* it was discovered that the executive director had given herself thousands of dollars over the past three years in bonuses, the board decides it must enact certain controls and monitor the finances more carefully. *After* the youth pastor is arrested for abusing a student, the church enacts new prevention policies and monitoring practices. *After* reports of bullying by a leader, someone decides it might be a good idea to have a whistle-blower policy or grievance process.

Too often, the people around a leader abdicate their responsibilities until after they've been caught flat-footed. Only then do they scramble to put in place the auditing practices that could have prevented the disaster in the first place.

In David's example above, his self-applied instruments for confronting the four propositions of risk were generally serving him well, but they were distorted at the time by his fatigue and possible boredom, and he was not inviting anyone else to help him generate or press into new perspectives. His self-applied instruments were helpful but insufficient in exposing and confronting what was necessary in order to produce an optimal decision. It was only when he invited externally applied instruments to the decision that the best course of action became clear.

As a leader, you may be accountable to a board of elders or directors who provide this form of oversight. In our experience, it feels a lot better when you *offer* to be audited or monitored than when someone else imposes it. It builds mutual trust and confidence when you can say to a board, boss, spouse, or friend, "Here's what I've been up to. Here's what I'm thinking. Take a look." Conversely, it tends to diminish trust and confidence when a board, boss, spouse or friend must ask, "What have you been up to? Let me see." So actively invite accountability, invite an audit—around your desires, opportunities, use of power, and expectations.

As you apply the DOPE Model to any risk-based decision—as you work your way through the four propositions of risk—you may wish to include at least one instrument of each of these four types: self-awareness, self-discipline, transparency, and audit.

Approach these tasks with a spirit of humility, an appreciation for your vulnerability to sin, and an attitude of full submission to God. "The LORD's light penetrates the human spirit, exposing every hidden motive" (Prov. 20:27).

Before arriving at your final decision, be sure to mitigate the effects of self-interest. Self-interest can tag along with each proposition, threatening to derail you at any point in your decision-making process, potentially leading to destructive risks that can bring harm upon yourself and the people you lead and love. Respect your vulnerability to sin, particularly your pride.

And finally, ask God to help you summon the courage to confront the "temporal fear" that can hold you back from taking healthy risks. We define temporal fear as a concern with worldly or temporal consequences, painful or pleasurable, over eternal ones. Remember that God is in control, he knows what he's doing, and he loves you no matter what. And eternal consequences are the ones that matter most.

CHAPTER 13

THE NEED TO ESCAPE

As a leader, you set the tone for your organization or unit. You are in the public eye. You carry more responsibility (or blame) than others for how things turn out. You challenge others to fulfill the mission and honor the core values. You probably feel some pressure to be a role model. To maintain credibility and effectiveness, it is important that you "walk the walk" and remain "on your game."

All of that can suck the life out of you. With the weight of that responsibility, you may feel the need to escape the pressure from time to time. To get some privacy. To be a nobody. To be unburdened.

There is something to be said for the rejuvenating effects of healthy escape. That might take the form of relaxing hobbies (gardening, fly-fishing, painting), thrilling hobbies (skydiving, racing, alligator wrestling), periodic personal retreats, disciplined use of vacation time, or some other means of "getting away from it all." Escape is sometimes needed from the pressures of being in the spotlight, getting results, being on your game, looking like you have it all together. We encourage healthy escape, where you generate circumstances or opportunities that allow you to flee the spotlight, relax, be yourself, and rejuvenate.

• • •

There is a fine line between healthy and unhealthy escape. Unhealthy escape takes privacy to an extreme and may increase your vulnerability to destructive risk-based behavior. The concept of privacy includes elements of separation (being apart from others, secluded, or free from unwanted intrusions and disturbances) and of concealment, secrecy, or anonymity.

While some measure of *privacy* can be good and healthy, the *secrecy and anonymity* elements of privacy often fuel bad behavior. People tend to behave badly on anonymous surveys, when offering commentary under their social media identities, and behind the wheel of a car with tinted windows. When our identity or behavior can be hidden or concealed, we tend to behave badly and take foolish risks.

• • •

Early on in leadership, I (David) began to feel the need to escape. It seems that every five or six weeks I long to get away. For years, when our kids were younger and still in school, my typical "day off" was on Wednesday. One of my favorite "day off" activities was to go to the movies with Ruth. We would catch the early afternoon matinee, which was not only cheaper, but it also meant there was a good chance that Ruth and I would be the only two people in the theater. It was like our own private showing.

I loved our movie dates. Though I enjoyed a good action flick, the movie itself wasn't important. Just the fact that I could get away from all other humans, turn off the phone, sit next to Ruth, and eat from our bottomless bucket of popcorn made the date worthwhile. It was my bimonthly form of escape.

As my responsibilities grew in unison with the growth of LCBC Church, my need and my desire to escape seem to grow proportionately. Additionally, I found that it was important for the rest of our staff to have time away from me. They needed to know they could make their own wise decisions. I needed to lessen their dependency on me.

So, with our kids grown and out of the house, my mode of escape advanced from monthly movie dates with Ruth to travel with Ruth. "With Ruth" being the operative words. By tacking a few days on to business trips or simply heading out on our own pleasure trips, the opportunity to disconnect from work and others has been invaluable for me. But it is always with Ruth. I don't go to movies without Ruth, nor do I travel alone (and now almost never without Ruth).

I realize that my situation might be unique. You may not have the luxury of traveling with your spouse. The funding for your spouse to travel with you might not be available from your employer or your own personal account. And if both spouses work or you have young children at home, it may not be practical to take time off to travel together all the time.

If this is the case for you and your spouse, consider the following measures when you are away from each other:

- Avoid situations where you will be alone with someone of the opposite sex.
- Create transparency with your spouse about where you are at any given time. You can do this by committing to texting or calling frequently. Make a habit of telling them what's on your schedule, what you did, who you were with. You might even consider activating the locator service on your phone so they can see where you are at any given moment. That may sound extreme, but is it really? I (Rob) always tell my wife, Marita, exactly where I'll be if I'm hunting alone in the woods, because things can go wrong out there. If I'm willing

to do that, why not let her know where I'll be in other situations too?

- Create transparency around your spending with your spouse. Make sure you both have easy access to your budget and your banking and credit card accounts. If you can both readily see when money comes in and how it goes out (by keeping receipts for cash expenditures and reviewing charges on credit cards), the temptation to spend on secret indulgences is reduced.

- Don't hang out with people who might encourage bad behavior. If your travel companions are heading out to a bar for a night of gawking and a few drinks, don't join them. Just don't put yourself in that kind of situation.

It's quite possible you and your spouse do not share a love for the same escape hobbies. For example, fishing and hunting are hobbies I (Rob) enjoy. My wife, Marita, likes fishing enough that we often fish together, but sometimes, I will just fish by myself, with a male buddy, or with a group of friends (which might include males and females). Marita is never going to hunt. She despises cold weather and can think of nothing more boring than sitting around waiting for an animal to walk by. But she loves dogs. So she sometimes joins me on bird hunts, where she can manage our dog as we walk the fields together.

● ● ●

I (Rob) sometimes intentionally conceal my identity as a human being by wearing camouflaged clothing. I do this when hunting, with the aim of becoming unrecognizable as a predator to my prey, so I can get close enough to shoot accurately and thereby put food on the table.

On one October afternoon, I decked myself out in full camo—only my eyes were uncovered—and ventured out to the woods to hunt deer. I worked my way about twenty feet up an oak tree in my climber. (This type of tree stand is exactly what it sounds like. You carry it into the woods and use the stand itself to scamper up a tree.)

I wanted to look like part of the tree if a deer should walk by, so I sat very still, trying to move nothing but my eyes. After an hour or so, I noticed a hawk was studying me from another tree about thirty yards away. It kept cranking its neck and making periodic hawk calls. After a few more minutes, it did a flyby for a closer look, and then perched on another tree, continuing to study and screech at me. The hawk made a few more flybys, but nothing very threatening. Even so, I was getting a little nervous. To my relief, it flew a bit further away, seemingly ready to leave me alone.

But then I saw the raptor leave its perch and head straight at me with its talons dangling. I've seen enough nature documentaries to know it was hungry and I was in trouble. My instinct was to raise my arms, using my crossbow to shield myself from the impending attack. I'm not proud to say that I also let out an involuntary cowardly shriek as I stood. Once I did that, the raging raptor veered away and abandoned the hunt.

I'm no biologist, but my guess is that my nemesis saw my eyes moving, but because of my camouflage, could not assess the size or shape of my body. He or she must have suspected I was a tasty rodent or bird and decided to move in for the snatch and grab. Only when I revealed myself as a large mammal did the hawk abandon the chase. I was concealed because I wanted to prey upon a deer. I hadn't considered the unintended consequences of my concealment—namely, that I might turn from predator to prey.

Whenever you or I operate in concealment, in hiding, or under a veil of anonymity, we open ourselves up to becoming prey and experiencing unintended and not so pleasurable consequences.

I have a generally good-natured friend who admits he is an irritable driver. He told me of a time, when heading home from a church function, that another motorist pulled very close to his bumper at a traffic light and sounded their horn immediately after the light turned green. Incensed and eager to retaliate, my friend decided to crawl along as slowly as possible so the other motorist might think twice before behaving so rudely in the future. Wanting to leave no doubt about his displeasure, he enhanced the communication package by adding an aggressive hand gesture. At the next light, the other driver pulled alongside him. Glancing over, my friend recognized her as the pastor's fiancé. She knew it was him all along, and was just joking around trying to get his attention. Oops.

On a more sober note, I once worked in a professional capacity with a prominent community leader who struggled with a pornography addiction. This was a well-respected person who accomplished a great deal of good for others in his day-to-day work. But he had a problem. He didn't need anyone to tell him his behavior was wrong. He knew that already.

His work sometimes required him to drive to another part of the state, where the most direct route to his destination took him through a cluster of "gentlemen's clubs" and adult video stores about an hour's drive from his hometown. Because it was away from his community, this man could indulge his addiction anonymously—or so he thought. He told me of a "wake-up call" he experienced one day.

As he was exiting a viewing booth, he bumped into a client of his, who was himself a fairly prominent figure in their home community. They glanced at each other in recognition, and silently went their separate ways. My client told me of the immediate shame and fear that overwhelmed him at that moment, as his cover was blown. He decided that day to take a different route from that point forward, deleting an option that enabled him to feed an unhealthy desire.

Whenever you or I operate in concealment, in hiding, or under a veil of anonymity, we just might be up to something that has potential harmful consequences to other people (or to our own reputations, if our identity were to become known).

What if everybody knew? What if your spouse witnessed you joking around with that attractive coworker? What if your subordinate saw you charge that *mostly personal but arguably work-related expense* on your company credit card? Would you have some explaining to do? If so, it's time to limit your opportunities to risk. To restrict the range of "What is available?"

What if the things you do in the dark (in secret, anonymously) were brought into the light? Pornography, drinking, exposure to violent or sexually explicit movies, visits to massage parlors, gambling, time spent alone with attractive coworkers. What if your checkbook were laid bare before others, so that they knew the products and services you're consuming?

So, while we encourage constructive escape, we recommend against escape-behavior that allows us to operate in secrecy or anonymity. If your answer to "What if everybody knew?" is something to the effect that you would be embarrassed or ashamed, then you can be pretty sure that your constructive escape is not so constructive after all, and that it's time to find a new means of escape or a new hobby.

CONCLUSION

DESIGNED TO SAIL

The average Major League Baseball player will walk up to home plate to face an opposition pitcher four times per game, all for the opportunity to take a risk to get on base and eventually score a run. This season, currently the best hitting team in all of MLB has a collective batting average of .265 percent. The best hitter in the league at the moment is batting .329, and the best hitter of all time, Ty Cobb, had a lifetime average of .366. Which means the very best batters came up empty two out of every three times at bat.

This year, the best shooting team in the National Basketball Association made 49.1 percent of their shots as a team. Which means every time the Brooklyn Nets took a risk and shot the ball, there was a less than 50/50 chance the ball would go through the net.

But basketball players keep shooting the ball. And baseball players keeping taking at-bats. Because getting hits and making baskets require taking risks. And even though professional athletes are paid for being the best in the world in their particular sport, they are far from perfect at taking risks. They fail more than they succeed. But to be the best requires taking risks.

To increase their odds of success, athletes exercise great discipline honing their craft and improving their skills. But they will still fail more than they will succeed. But to be the best requires taking risks.

As leaders, you and I are called to take risks. Exercising the discipline to master the DOPE Model will improve your skills in calculating risks and increase your odds of taking successful risks. But like basketball and baseball players, there are times that you'll risk and fail. Yet basketball players keep shooting the ball, and baseball players keep taking at-bats, and leaders keep taking risks. It's what we do. Don't be deterred.

● ● ●

As my (David's) daughter, Ashleigh, was entering her teenage years, I decided we needed a "bonding" activity. With a small lake just a few miles from our home, we decided to try sailing together. I shelled out a few hundred dollars and Ashleigh and I invested in a sailboat. It wasn't really a sailboat; it was more like a surfboard that happened to have a sail attached to it. So, don't think sailboat—think surfboard. And Ashleigh named our surfboat, "Dash-Diddly."

This was not my first experience with sailing. That came while Ruth and I were on a five-day vacation in Jamaica. One morning I decided to take sailing lessons—what better place to learn to sail than in the crystal-clear waters of the Caribbean! There was not a great deal of instruction associated with my lesson—meaning after standing and looking at the catamaran for a few minutes next to my instructor—he said I was ready to go solo. But rather than go out solo, I tried to coax Ruth into going with me. Wisely, she refused.

With the wind at my back, I headed away from the shore and out to sea. The clear water, the Caribbean breeze, the bright sun . . . all was fine until I realized that if I didn't make a turn soon my next stop would be Cuba. Very quickly I discovered that I had not been adequately schooled in the art of sailing.

As I maneuvered and prepared the little catamaran for a turn, it became apparent that I had not accurately factored the force of the wind into my turn. So when the full force of the wind caught the sail it threw me off balance and sent me flailing into the water as the boat lay completely over on its side.

Fortunately, my instructor had been keeping a close eye on me. More specifically, he had been keeping an eye on *his* boat. Jumping in a powerboat, he came out and helped me right my boat; then he helped me board my boat; then he took me on the ride of shame as he towed me back to the shore. Needless to say,

I had little luck ever talking Ruth into sailing with me from that moment on!

But Ashleigh was young and adventurous (some might argue she was naive and overly trusting), plus she hadn't been there to experience my Jamaican sail (fail). So, as Ashleigh and I headed out to Speedwell Forge Lake for our first sailing experience together, we were both excited and nervous. Ashleigh was less nervous than excited. I, on the other hand, was more nervous than excited. After all, I knew that I knew very little about sailing. As I finished clipping on my life jacket, I pushed Ashleigh and Dash-Diddly into the water and away from the shore.

Ashleigh wasn't more than five feet from the shore when a park ranger pulled up in his truck and asked me to pull her back to shore. While writing up a $95 citation, he explained that both Ashleigh and I needed whistles on our life jackets before we could put Dash-Diddly back in the water.

Now armed with whistles, a few days later we headed back to Speedwell Forge for our second attempt at sailing. This time we were both on our surfboat and out about twenty feet from the shore when we noticed our friendly park ranger once again waving us back onto the shore. While writing up our second $95 citation, he explained that our surfboat needed a registration number and that number was to be posted visibly across the side of the surfboat. (Could've told us that the first time, no?)

A few days later, with our whistles attached to our life jackets and our registration number shining on the side of our surfboat, I glanced around for our friend, Mr. Park Ranger. With no park ranger in sight, Ashleigh and I crawled on to Dash-Diddly and quietly slid out into the water. The third time was the charm! With Ashleigh lying across the front and me seated on the back, we paddled out into the water, careful not to rock the boat and tip over.

Fifty feet into the lake, we faced the moment of decision: Do we play it safe by just paddling around the lake on our surfboat, or do we take a risk and let out the sail? With no sail, I could control the surfboat. With no sail we wouldn't go far, and we wouldn't go fast—really all we would do is drift. But it felt like I was in control, and there was little danger of flipping the boat.

There was risk involved in letting out the sail. I would give up control if I let out the sail, but sailboats are made to sail. So, with some fear and trepidation, we took a risk and let out the sail. As the breeze began to fill our sail, we started to move. We moved faster and faster, gliding across the water and experiencing a thrill we had never experienced before.

We laughed and we squealed as we leaned into the wind— and yes, we turned our surfboat over and landed in the water multiple times. But it was amazing! And for the next several years Ash and I would head back out to Speedwell Forge to do what Dash-Diddly was designed to do: take risks, let out the sails, and sail.

You and I are designed to sail. God has designed you to take risks. Will you, wisely, take them?

• • •

King Solomon, considered by God to be the wisest person on earth, stated in Proverbs 27:12, "A prudent person foresees danger and takes precautions. The simpleton goes blindly on and suffers the consequences." Proudly assuming success ignores the dangers of taking foolish risks and invites its negative consequences.

Our prayer is that you will put up your sails and embrace risks. And as you do, may you hear the words of Jesus as spoken by the master to his servant:

> "Well done, my good and faithful servant. You have been faithful in handing this small amount [risk], so now I will give you many more responsibilities [risks]. Let's celebrate together!" (Matt. 25:21)

NOTES

1. "Super Bowl LII Like You Have Never Seen It Before" (NFL Films, posted to YouTube on February 12, 2018), https://www.youtube.com/watch?v=x_RHOB9xkqo.

2. Jonathan Haidt, *The Righteous Mind: Why Good People Are Divided by Politics and Religion* (New York: Pantheon Books, 2012), 97.

3. Haidt, *The Righteous Mind*, 106.

4. Dacher Keltner, *The Power Paradox: How We Gain and Lose Influence* (New York: Penguin Press, 2016).

5. Jim Collins, *Good to Great: Why Some Companies Make the Leap . . . and Others Don't* (New York: HarperCollins, 2001), 35.

6. *Newsweek*, July 23, 2021, https://www.newsweek.com/americas-got-talent-2021-season-16-golden-buzzer-howie-simon-heidi-sofia-terry-crews-1596717.

7. https://www.quoteslyfe.com/quote/In-order-to-find-the-edge-you-275227

8. John Cherwa, "The Kingmaker: Don Shula," *Orlando Sentinel*, August 24, 2007, https://www.orlandosentinel.com/news/os-xpm-2007-08-24-dolphinsking24-story.html.

9. https://www.goodreads.com/quotes/613433-i-think-we-should-follow-a-simple-rule-if-we

10. Glenna Whitley, "The Second Coming of Billy Weber," *D Magazine*, July 1989, https://www.dmagazine.com/publications/d-magazine/1989/july/the-second-coming-of-billy-weber/.

11. Ibid.

12. Ibid.